SECRET
BARCELONA

Rocio Sierra Carbonell and Carlos Mesa

We have taken great pleasure in drawing up
Secret Barcelona and hope that through its guidance
you will, like us, continue to discover unusual,
hidden or little-known aspects of the city.
Descriptions of certain places are accompanied
by thematic sections highlighting historical details
or anecdotes as an aid to understanding the city in
all its complexity.
Secret Barcelona also draws attention to the
multitude of details found in places that we
may pass every day without noticing. These are
an invitation to look more closely at the urban
landscape and, more generally, a means of seeing
our own city with the curiosity and attention that
we often display while travelling elsewhere …

Comments on this guidebook and its contents,
as well as information on places we may not have
mentioned, are more than welcome and will enrich
future editions.
Don't hesitate to contact us:
• Éditions Jonglez, 17, boulevard du Roi,
  78000 Versailles, France
• E-mail: info@jonglezpublishing.com

CONTENTS

CONTENTS

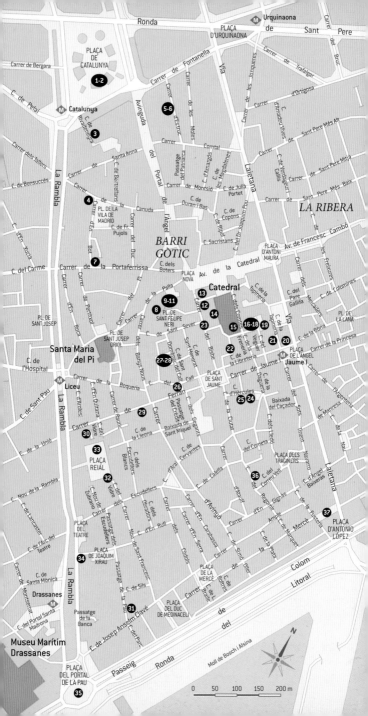

BARRI GÒTIC

STATUE OF THE BLACK MADONNA OF MONTSERRAT

❶

Plaça de Catalunya
• Metro: Catalunya

> *A miniature Black Madonna saved from the anarchists*

As an Eastern proverb says, the protruding nail attracts the hammer. Passing unnoticed and blending in is sometimes the best way to survive.

The Virgin of Montserrat in Plaça de Catalunya is a good example. The story goes that she was saved from the wave of anticlerical fervour and iconoclasm unleashed by the anarchists in Barcelona at the beginning of the Civil War (1936–39), as they failed to even notice her. Otherwise the statue would probably have been melted down or smashed with a sledgehammer. She survived unscathed to comfort many Catholics who murmured a clandestine prayer each time they passed. Today she still stands beside the stone benches lining the square near the Aerobus stop.

The Montserrat sculpture by Eusebi Arnau (1864–1934), of which the Virgin forms part, was installed in 1928 during the work carried out in Plaça de Catalunya for the International Exposition of 1929. The sculpture commemorates Brother Joan Garí, who according to legend was tempted by the devil and committed a horrific murder in the 9th century. Repentant, he wandered in the mountains of Montserrat, becoming a hermit, eating herbs and drinking rainwater to obtain God's forgiveness, which was granted when the Virgin appeared to him in a mountain cave.

ROTARY CLUB SYMBOLISM ❷

Plaça de Catalunya
• Metro: Catalunya

Rotarians in Plaça de Catalunya

In 1862, Barcelona City Council planned to renovate the site that would become Plaça de Catalunya. However, because of the Universal Exposition of 1888, official permission was not granted until 1889 after a competition had been held. It was won by the Freemason Pere Falqués (his streetlights in Barcelona's Passeig de Sant Joan bear the well-known symbol of the compass and set square).

The first stage of the development (two major routes forming an X with a circular intersection) began in 1902.

The second stage went ahead for the Universal Exposition of 1929: the first project by the Modernist architect Josep Puig i Cadafalch (1923) was interrupted during the construction of the metro and then ground to a halt under the dictatorship of Primo de Rivera. Francesc Nebot took over from Puig and drew up an almost identical project, replacing the obelisk in the original plan by a small colonnaded temple that in the end was never built – hence Nebot's resignation. He was replaced by Joaquim Llansó, Josep Cabestany and Nicolau Maria Rubió i Tudurí, the latter being a known Freemason. The square was inaugurated by Alfonso XIII on 2 November 1927.

In 1905, the Freemason lawyer Paul Harris had founded the elite organization of the Rotary Club with three of his friends, Gustavus H. Loer, Silvester Schiele and Hiram E. Shorey, whereupon Harris was expelled from the Freemasons for setting up an elitist club that failed to respect the concept of equality dear to Masons. To be a Rotarian, members had to fulfil certain financial conditions that were beyond the reach of certain classes, while anyone should be able to join the Masonic ranks regardless of social status.

In 1929, the Spanish Church issued a document based on Pope Pius XI's Encyclical Letter *Quas Primas* of 1925, warning the faithful and urging them not to be part of this association whose precepts were inconsistent with the spirit of the Church.

The wheel was the symbol of the Rotary Club from the outset: it was first drawn by a Rotarian from Chicago, the metal engraver Montague Bear, who sketched a simple wheel with a cloud of dust at its base to give the idea of movement. The wheel represented "Civilization and Movement". However, most of the early clubs created their own logos for publications and correspondence. Finally, in 1922, it was decided that all Rotary Clubs should bear the same insignia. In 1923, the current serrated wheel with twenty-four cogs and six spokes was approved by Rotary International.

If you look carefully at the layout of Plaça de Catalunya, you'll see in it the first symbol of the Rotary Club, before the addition of the twenty-four cogs. This suggests that some of those who contributed to the original project (we don't yet know who) had links to the Rotarian movement, which was beginning to spread throughout Europe.

HEADQUARTERS OF THE KNIGHTS OF THE HOLY SEPULCHRE

❸

Parish church of Santa Anna - Passeig de Rivadeneyra, 3
• Metro: Catalunya
• Tel: 93 301 3576 • Open daily, 9.00–20.00

> ### *The knights have not left the building*

The church of Santa Anna, just off Plaça de Catalunya, seems isolated and even a little secretive. During the Napoleonic invasion it was closed by the French, and it is said to have been used as a refuge for Catalan resistance against the invaders. It is a secluded and timeless place away from the crowds, accessed by crossing a little square surrounded on all sides by modern buildings. Its two doors, one leading to Carrer de Santa Anna and the other to Passeig de Rivadeneyra, are closed at night. A beautiful cloistered garden and a chapter house are still attached to the church, which is part of a former convent.

The main chapel – also known as the Chapel of Forgiveness – is home to a representation of the Holy Sepulchre. It was considered the most important sanctuary in the church because of a papal bull that granted indulgences and forgave the sins of all the faithful who turned up between vespers on 16 March and sunset the next day and then did the appropriate penance. These "Santa Anna Pardons" had the same value as those obtained by going on a pilgrimage to the Holy Sepulchre of Jerusalem.

Symbolizing this pilgrimage, the scallop shell emblem of Saint James was carved into the stone walls of the church, particularly outside the Chapel of Forgiveness.

Currently, the mother house in Spain is the Collegiate church of Santa María of Calatayud (Zaragoza), where the knights hold their general chapter meeting at least once a year. There are two lieutenancies: the Calatayud and Santa Anna in Barcelona, where the chapters of Catalonia and Aragon still

hold their annual assemblies. The Knights of the Holy Sepulchre attend these meetings dressed in their ancient regalia.

Of particular note inside the church is the tomb of Miquel Boera, born in Sant Feliu de Guíxols. He took part in the North Africa campaigns between 1510 and 1522 in the service of the viceroy of Naples, Ramón de Cardona. He served as a general at the Battle of Ravenna in 1512, during the reign of Charles I, and was rewarded with the rank of captain-general. As he was a renowned Knight of the Holy Sepulchre, his tomb was moved to the old church of Santa Anna.

To emphasize the Order's connection to the Patriarch of Jerusalem, a patriarchal double cross was displayed on the façade of their churches. A cross potent, with crossbars or "crutches" at the four ends (five crosses in all, recalling Christ's wounds), features on the knights' coats and capes. On certain occasions in the church of Santa Anna, the Knights of the Holy Sepulchre, in full ceremonial dress, mark the first Monday of each month before the astonished gaze of passers-by.

ORDER OF THE HOLY SEPULCHRE OF JERUSALEM

The Order of the Holy Sepulchre of Jerusalem is a military and religious chivalric order of knighthood thought to have been founded by Duke Godfrey of Bouillon, victor of the First Crusade in 1099 at Jerusalem, or even, according to other sources, by Charlemagne (in 808). With its headquarters in Rome at Sant'Onofrio monastery on Janiculum Hill, the order has thirty-five branches around the world. There are some 18,000 Knights and Ladies of the Holy Sepulchre, whose principal aim is to encourage and propagate their faith in the Holy Land, under the authority of the pope. The order owes its name to the Holy Cross of Jerusalem, the sanctuary built around the supposed site of Christ's crucifixion and the place where he is thought to have been buried and resurrected.

Today the order runs forty-four Catholic schools in and around Jerusalem, bringing together some 15,000 pupils, both Christian and Muslim.

In France, the order is the guardian of the holy relic of Christ's crown of thorns (see *Secret Paris* in this series of guides).

THE CROSS OF THE ORDER OF THE HOLY SEPULCHRE OF JERUSALEM

The insignia of the order is the red Jerusalem cross or cross potent (with crossbars), surrounded by four smaller crosses. These five crosses now serve as a reminder of the five wounds of Christ on the Cross, even though

they originally signified that the Word of Christ had spread in four directions around the world.

The symbolism is also of resurrection.

The colour red, representing life, strength and blood, was chosen to commemorate the wounds inflicted on Christ.

In the East, the cross is golden, symbolising the immense value of Christ's Passion.

CLUB ATENEU BARCELONÉS ④

Carrer de la Canuda, 6
• Metro: Catalunya • Tel: 93 343 6121 • Open daily 9.00–22.30
• www.ateneubcn.org/
• Members only. Monthly subscription (€21) gives access to all Ateneu services: library, meeting rooms, cafeteria
• If you only want to visit the romantic gardens, you can ask for a special pass at reception

A secret garden and library

The Sabassona palace was commissioned by Josep Francesc de Llupià, baron of Sabassona, in 1779. Designed by the architect Pau Mas and listed as a national monument, the neoclassical building was renovated several times in the course of the 20th century. Other than its architectural importance (notably the superb entrance door on Carrer de la Canuda), the palace features the paintings of Françesc Pla ("El Vigatà"), who in the mid-18th century made his name as interior decorator of stately homes and private mansions.

He also designed the romantic garden located 5 metres above street level, a superbly relaxing spot with a wide variety of plants and flowers, in the heart of the Barrio Gótico.

Since 1907 the palace has been home to Ateneu Barcelonés, which defines itself as "a haven of tolerance, liberty and national culture."

Apart from the romantic garden and a collection of artworks, the Ateneu has a fantastic library of over 1,000 m2, open to any students and researchers with an interest in Catalonian history, politics, and society.

Recent renovation work has returned the library to the splendour of its early years (it was founded in 1860).

The repository contains over 300,000 volumes, a great number of incunabula, tens of thousands of historical documents, and special editions dating from the 14th to the 18th centuries. It is one of the most important national collections in Spain.

WATERING THE HORSES

The drinking fountains where tourists and local residents come to refresh themselves today were, until the late 1950s, intended for draught animals that pulled the carts carrying merchandise into the city. They were to be found at ?? Vila i Vilá, 40 Carrer del Consell de Cent, and at the junction of Portal de l'Ángel and Carrer del Cucurulla. The oldest (14th century) is the one in Cucurulla.

The errand boys responsible for delivering goods in the port area, and in particular the neighbourhoods of El Born and Poblenou, would stop at the water troughs to let the animals refresh themselves, usually leaving them tied up while they themselves drank eau-de-vie or wine in the bars nearby.

KABBALISTIC PLAQUES IN CARRER D'ESTRUC

❺

Carrer d'Estruc, 14
• Metro: Catalunya

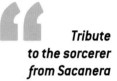

*Tribute
to the sorcerer
from Sacanera*

Two strange plaques, one at No. 14 (opposite) and the other at No. 22 (see following double-page spread), can be seen on the walls of the intriguing Carrer d'Estruc.

The plaque at No. 14, affixed in the late 20th century by Catalan occultist Ricardo Bru, consists of an inscription that reads: "At the beginning of the 15th century people called this street Astruc Sacanera, as a tribute to the astrologer or sorcerer from Sacanera. Astruc is a medicinal herb and an ancient word for astrologers or sorcerers. Here was sold the viper's stone, with properties against rabies and bites."

The witch doctor Astruc Sacanera was indeed famous for selling a special powder and stone as an antidote to insect and snake bites, even the most poisonous. Note that the word *astruc* (together with the variants *struch*, *estruch* and *estruc*), probably through its association with Sacanera, is also the name of a medicinal herb and a term applied in the Middle Ages to sorcerers and healers, while the Catalan word *astrugança* means "luck".

Pliny the Elder refers to this remedy in his *Natural History* under the name *Ovum anguinum*, a kind of snake extract that set as hard as stone and was used by the Druids of Gaul as a treatment for venomous bites.

Apparently corresponding to a bone from the serpent's head, the viper's stone had to be applied to the wound. It was supposed to stick to the skin immediately and absorb the poison, after which it mysteriously dropped off. This method is still used today in many parts of the world, where it is known as the *black stone* or *snake stone*.

At the top right and bottom left of this inscription, Bru also had two medallions engraved as talismans incorporating Kabbalistic signs and Hebrew magic formulas, meant to protect the plaque and more generally the street. The Kabbalah, an esoteric Hebrew tradition, is not limited to study of the scriptures. It also involves, as in this case, practical knowledge of medicine and alchemy as well as Operative magic, which invokes and communicates directly with beings from invisible worlds.

MYSTICAL PLAQUE AT NO. 22 ❻

Carrer d'Estruc, 22
• Metro: Catalunya

> ### *Another protective talisman*

Until the late 20th century, Carrer d'Estruc had a bookshop stocking anthropological curiosities that had always belonged to the Estruch family. It sold all kinds of strange artefacts that the owner had brought back from his extensive travels. Eventually this unique bookshop closed and so the last vestige of this mystical Jewish family disappeared.

A souvenir still remains in the form of a plaque at No. 22, which indicates exactly where the famous "viper's stone" was sold (see previous double-page spread).

The plaque is another mystical talisman that shows a snake at the centre, linked to the bite remedy (see opposite) and the Hebrew names used to invoke the powers of the Most High (*Tetragrammaton Jehova*) and the Angel of the Saviour (*Jelah Emmanuel*).

Note also that the numbers of buildings along the street appear on the plaque, bordered by Kabbalistic symbols that are actually magic seals, common in the practices of esoteric rabbis of the Middle Ages. They were inspired by the spellbooks of the medieval *Clavicula Salomonis* (Key of Solomon), composed of thirty-six charms formed from the sacred names of Judaism, the names of archangels and astrological signs. According to this tradition, the symbols represented here acted as a protective talisman for the neighbourhood.

SYMBOLISM OF THE SNAKE

Symbolically, the snake represents both death and evil that must be overcome by a virtuous life in the service of others, but also renaissance, as can be read in the Bible (Book of Numbers), where although land snakes sent by God were thought to have destroyed many in Israel, the chosen people found life again through the snake, following the instructions the Lord gave to Moses: *Then the Lord sent venomous snakes among them; they bit the people and many Israelites died. The people came to Moses and said, "We sinned when we spoke against the Lord and against you. Pray that the Lord will take the snakes away from us." So Moses prayed for the people. The Lord said to Moses, "Make a snake and put it up on a pole; anyone who is bitten can look at it and live." So Moses made a bronze snake and put it up on a pole. Then when anyone was bitten by a snake and looked at the bronze snake, they lived.* (Numbers 21: 6–9).

Thus the snake nailed to a Tau Cross became the symbol of the Kabbalah. Recovery from its bite meant the domination of the "venomous snake", spiritual enlightenment through the awakening of the inner light, as Moses was bathed in light coming down from Mount Sinai after meeting with the Lord Jehovah. The Hebrews called those who were spiritually enlightened *nahas*, similar to the Hindu *nagas*. The two terms mean "serpent" and in this case the Serpent of Wisdom that heals, illuminates and grants immortality to whoever looks upon it.

ESTRUC, THE FIRST CATALAN VAMPIRE

Although popular belief suggests that vampirism has its roots in Transylvania, the modern region of Ampurias (Emporion), near Girona, was the legendary setting for a terrifying story of vampires – *estruga* in Old Catalan. The word *estruga* comes from *estriga*, a Slavic vampire with two hearts and two souls.

The apparition of a vampire count dates from the reign of Peter II ("The Catholic"), around 1212, at the time of the ongoing conflicts between the Crown of Aragon and Catalonia against the French kings, who were attempting to seize Occitania.

Ampurias was a hotbed of intrigue and struggles against the Castilians and the English (allies of King Alfonso, enemies of Peter the Catholic), without forgetting the Navarrese who regularly rose up against Aragon.

General Estruc was a remarkable warrior who always fought for the Crown of Aragon. When getting on in years he was sent to Llers, a small town near Figueras, the home of paganism. The 12th-century Catalans were at the time still practising the ancient Iberian cults predating Christianity. General Estruc forced the farmers of the region to embrace the Christian faith and brutally suppressed their ancestral forms of worship in which magic and the occult held pride of place.

This repression explains why Estruc was cursed by his victims and after his death the rejuvenated count rose from his tomb as a vampire, spreading terror throughout Catalonia.

Another version of the story is that he was reborn among the living dead because he refused to allow one of his soldiers to marry his daughter. The rejected suitor poisoned her, casting a spell to bring her back to life transformed into an insatiable bloodsucker.

Whichever version you prefer, General Estruc – who was ennobled shortly before his death – emerged at night to drink the blood of his victims, seducing and raping young girls of marriageable age and then abandoning them when they became pregnant. Nine months later, little monsters came into the world stillborn because vampires can have no progeny.

So the reign of King Alfonso II was marked by unrest and intrigue and people were genuinely terrified. They were afraid to go out at night and armed themselves with garlic and crucifixes as protection against this Nosferatu. Nobody could sleep in peace until a former nun found the tomb of Count Estruc and drove a stake through his heart, thereby removing the curse forever.

But the memory of the vampire persisted, giving rise to the saying *"tenir malastruc"* or *"mala astrugancia"* to refer to someone who has no luck. It is said that the descendants of Count Estruc, seen as the children from hell, had to flee Llers and came to settle in Barcelona, where they acquired the street that bears their name.

MASONIC SCULPTURE

Carrer de la Portaferrissa, 11
• Metro: Liceu

Freemasons at Portaferrissa

On the façade of No. 11 Carrer de la Portaferrissa, above the door, is a sculptural group clearly of Masonic inspiration showing two children with a triangle set on a pile of bricks between them.

The child on the right has his right hand on the triangle and holds two rulers in his left hand, while the child leaning on the bricks has a trowel in his left hand and a compass in his right.

A document dating from 1867 in the Historic Archives of the City of Barcelona contains the planning permission for this building, designed by architect Domingo Sitjas. It is said that because the sculpture of the children was not in the original plans, probably to avoid attracting the attention of the authorities and the clergy of the time, the Guardia Civil did not demolish the building, having seen no trace of it in the archives.

Freemasonry has always been seen as a secret initiatory order, both philanthropic and philosophical in nature. According to both male and female members, the Masonic aim is to seek the truth and stimulate the intellectual and moral development of humanity, thus creating a more just and perfect society.

Such is the cryptic message of this sculpture, on a building that probably hosted a Masonic lodge in the 19th century, perhaps even in the early 20th century. The two children have the double attributes of innocence and purity. The pile of bricks topped by the triangle alludes to the edification of the new man and the new enlightened society by the divine presence of the Most Holy Trinity, which in the Masonic hierarchy is represented by the three basic degrees of master, companion and apprentice, in correlation with the theological principles of Father, Son and Holy Spirit. God the Father transmits wisdom to the master Mason, God the Son gives strength to the companion Mason and God the Holy Spirit inspires beauty in the apprentice Mason.

The child on the right also represents the master carpenter and the child on the left the master stonemason: the carpenter and the stonemason, plank by plank and stone by stone, raise the ideal temple of the new man that Freemasonry is creating on Earth, both mentally and morally.

For more on the Masonic symbolism of ruler, trowel and compass, as well as Franco and Freemasonry, see following double-page spread.

WHEN FRANCO TWICE ASKED TO JOIN THE FREEMASONS

Lluís Companys, the last Republican president of the Generalitat de Catalunya, was initiated into Freemasonry on 2 May 1922 in the Lealtad lodge in Barcelona. He was executed by firing squad on the orders of General Franco on 15 October 1940 because of his Masonic associations.

On 15 September 1936, Franco signed his first decree against Freemasonry. What the official histories do not record is that in 1932, when he was a lieutenant-colonel, he had asked to enter the Lukus de Larraix lodge. That same year he made the same request at the Plus Ultra lodge in Madrid, where his brother Ramón Franco was a member. Not only was Franco's brother a Mason but he belonged to the Esquerra Republicana de Catalunya (a Catalan nationalist political party launched in 1931 to advocate a republic). Apparently he refused to vote in favour of Franco joining the Masons because "he was not an upstanding man, with good morals".

Franco took his revenge by commandeering all the lodges and having known Freemasons shot. He also wrote four anti-Masonic articles for the *ABC* newspaper under the pseudonym Jakim Boor (a reference to Jachin and Boaz, the two pillars at the entrance to Solomon's Temple) between 14 December 1946 and 3 May 1951.

On 1 October 1975, two months before his death, Franco again attacked the

Masons in a public speech in Madrid's Plaza de Oriente.

In 1976, during the transition of power, Rodolfo Martín Villa, Minister of the Interior, called President Adolfo Suárez to tell him: "I have two Freemasons here. What shall I do? Arrest them?" Suárez' response left him in no doubt: "Legalize them!" Since that day, Freemasonry has been legal in Spain.

Although Catholic Spain has never tolerated Freemasonry, which has always been harshly and violently repressed (in 1829, members of a Barcelona lodge were arrested and sentenced, one to the death penalty and the others to life imprisonment, while the Worshipful Master, lieutenant-colonel Gálvez, was hanged), today Barcelona is still home to the greatest number of Masons in Spain – over 1,500.

MASONIC SYMBOLISM OF THE SQUARE, TROWEL AND COMPASS

In Masonic symbolism, the set-square stands for rectitude, method and law, three principles symbolically supported by the angles of the triangle. In ancient Egypt, the god Ptah was shown with a rule in his hand to measure the Nile floods. So the 24 inch rule, which features in Masonic lodges as a working tool and a measure of time, indicates that we should not squander 24 hours a day in idle and selfish pursuits, but that 8 hours must be devoted to meditation, 8 more to work and the remaining 8 to leisure and rest, although the whole time should be applied to the service of humanity.

The trowel, a triangular flat shovel that stonemasons use to lay cement, is to Freemasonry the symbol of kindness, of conciliation and of silence. Its presence means that the feelings of goodwill that unite all Masons must be spread around. Brotherly love is the only cement that workers can use for building the temple of the Heavenly New Jerusalem (also known as the Eternal Orient) on Earth – the temple of human solidarity cemented by the selfless, caring and enlightened nature of one and all.

The compass, one of the principal Masonic symbols, is the emblem of measure and justice. The basic geometric shape that can be drawn with a compass is a circle around a central point. The ultimate solar symbol, the circle (infinity) is in congruence with the point (origin of any event or evolution). The relative and the absolute are thus represented by the action of the compass which, for its part, shows duality (the two legs) and unity (their junction). This is why Freemasonry adopted the compass as one of its major symbols and placed it on the altar of the lodge, enclosing the set-square to symbolize the macrocosm and the microcosm, above the Holy Book (Bible, Koran, Vedas, etc. according to the religion of the country where Freemasonry was established). This book signifies the wisdom that illuminates and directs both macrocosm and microcosm, and in particular the Masonic Order.

MUSEU DEL CALÇAT

8

Plaça de Sant Felip Neri, 5
Metro: Liceu
• Tel: 93 301 4533
• Open Tuesday to Sunday, 11.00–14.00
• Admission: €2.40

The biggest shoe in the world?

The Shoe Museum has an extraordinarily interesting collection of shoes from various periods. The items on display in this small and attractive space include a pair of giant sandals formerly used to signpost a shoe shop for illiterate passers-by.

Also featured are pointed-toe shoes that the French government banned as dangerous weapons in the 16th century, now back in fashion. You can see shepherd's sandals from the Roman Empire, and filigree metal-trimmed footwear from the 18th, 19th and early 20th centuries. In other showcases are satin pumps, work shoes, Turkish slippers and a musketeer's boots, showing how footgear evolved from the 1st century to the modern age.

Among the most unusual pieces are the cobbler's "last" that was used to make the shoes for the statue of Christopher Columbus at Portal de la Paz, and a replica of the giant shoe (1.22 metres) worn by the statue (56 metres from the ground to the top of its head).

THE LION OF SAINT MARK, PROTECTOR OF SHOEMAKERS

It is no coincidence that a bas-relief of a lion is carved on the wall of the Shoe Museum: the lion is the symbol of the Evangelist Saint Mark (the Gospel according to Mark begins with images of the desert where the lion reigns supreme), and the saint is also patron of the shoemakers' guild.

In Alexandria, in AD 42, a certain Ananios injured himself while repairing the footwear of the saint, who immediately and miraculously healed him. A legend was born.

The National Art Museum of Catalonia has a fresco from the apse of Sant Climent de Taüll church in the Pyrenees, in which Saint Mark's lion appears. The 12th-century artists were perhaps unfamiliar with lions, as this one looks rather like a bear ...

DISMANTLED STONE BY STONE

The building in which the Shoe Museum is located is the same one that in 1565 became home to the fraternity of Saint Mark the Evangelist and the shoemakers' guild. It used to stand in the Corribia road, before it was bombarded during the Civil War. The building was dismantled stone by stone and rebuilt on its present site during the postwar reconstruction of the Barri Gòtic by architect Adolf Florensa.

FLAMING HEART SCULPTURE ❾

Plaça de Sant Felip Neri
• Metro: Liceu

> *Reminder of the descent of the Holy Spirit ...*

In Plaça de Sant Felip Neri, above the gate surrounded by walls pockmarked with bullet holes (see p. 36), is a medallion depicting a heart erupting with tongues of fire. If this sounds familiar to the general public as a traditional Catholic symbol, in this case it refers to an episode in the life of Saint Philip Neri. Meditating in the catacombs of Rome, the saint was suddenly aware of a great light.

Just like Christ's Apostles, he too was receiving the Holy Spirit: a fireball entered his heart, which doubled in size on contact with the flames. This life-changing event is commemorated by the flaming heart symbol (further details opposite).

Plaça Sant Felip Neri is the location of the video clip for *My Immortal* by the band Evanescence.

SAINT PHILIP NERI, WHOSE HEART DOUBLED IN SIZE AS HE RECEIVED THE HOLY SPIRIT

Founder of the Congregation of the Oratory, also known as the Congregation of the Filippini after his forename, Saint Philip Neri (1515–1595) was often referred to as the joyful saint because of his cheerful disposition. Inspired by the early Christian communities, he wanted to anchor an intense spiritual life in a daily routine based on prayer (he was one of the first to gather around him laymen with whom he prayed), reading, meditating on the word of God and praising the Lord, mainly through chant and music. According to him, music was an excellent way of reaching people's hearts and bringing them closer to God, so he was one of the strongest supporters of the revival of sacred music.

In 1544, while the saint was praying in the catacombs of Saint Sebastian over the tombs of the early martyrs, his heart was suddenly seized with immense joy and an intense light shone down on him. Looking up, he saw a ball of fire that alighted on his mouth and entered his chest. On contact with the flames, his heart instantly expanded. The violence of the impact broke two of his ribs. The Holy Spirit had come to the saint, just as it did to the Apostles at Pentecost. In the 17th century, a scientific autopsy on his body confirmed that his heart was twice the size of a normal human heart. For the saint, nothing would be the same again. The beating of his heart was so strong that it could be heard some distance away and the heat that persistently consumed him meant that he could face the rigours of winter in his shirtsleeves. The symbol of the Congregation today, a heart in flames, is based on this episode of his life. While looking after the sick, poor and infirm, Saint Philip Neri also took care to spend time with young people in an attempt to stop them feeling bored or depressed. He often gathered a group around him and while always reminding them that life was to be lived joyfully, when the noise became too loud he is supposed to have said: "Quieten down a bit, my friends, if you can!"

His great spiritual gifts even allowed him to bring a young child momentarily back to life.

TRACES OF SHRAPNEL FROM THE CIVIL WAR ⑩

Plaça de Sant Felip Neri
• Metro: Liceu

Vestiges of the Civil War

The façades of several buildings in Plaça de Sant Felip Neri still show the traces of a tragic incident from the Civil War, during which around twenty residents were killed, most of them children. Historians now agree that these are shrapnel impacts from an aerial bombing by Italian planes that took place on 30 January 1938, although after the war Spanish Fascists tried to claim that they were the result of machine-gun fire from street executions carried out by the Communists. In this square, surely one of the most peaceful in the city centre, stands the church where the group of children had found refuge, never thinking that a shell would fall through the roof.

THE FACE OF GAUDÍ

⓫

Church of Sant Felip Neri
Plaça de Sant Felip Neri, 5
• Metro: Catalunya
• Tel: 93 317 3116
• Saturday and the day before festivals: 8.15–10.15 and 19.15–21.15
• Sunday: 10.00–14.00

*Gaudí
in the guise
of Saint Philip Neri*

At the age of 50, the architect Gaudí, who never wanted to be photographed or to appear in newspapers or magazines, agreed to pose for some portraits. One of them is in the Rosary Chapel of the Sagrada Família.

Every day, Gaudí went to the church of Sant Felip Neri to chat with the priest Lluís María de Valls. During the summer of 1902, he decided to pose for his friend, the painter Joan Llimona, for two works that are still kept in the church, one on each side of the presbytery. In the event, the artist chose the features and face of Gaudí to represent Saint Philip Neri in these two paintings,

On the right, Saint Philip Neri with the face of Gaudí is explaining Christian doctrine to some children on Rome's Gianicolo (Janiculum) hill. On the left, the saint, still depicted as Gaudí, is celebrating the Eucharist, the sacrament during which a miracle had occurred and the saint had begun to levitate.

Gaudí apparently said that he supported these works as the Eucharistic sacrifice would save such a sinful city as Barcelona.

The Baroque church of Sant Felip Neri was built between 1721 and 1752. Philip Neri, who was born in Florence on 22 July 1515 and died on 26 May 1595, founded the Congregation of the Oratory, which focused on youth, joy and music (for more on the saint, see *Secret Rome* in this series of guides).

SAINT LUCY'S YARDSTICK

12

Carrer del Bisbe, façade of Capella de Santa Lucia
next to Barcelona Cathedral
• Metro Jaume I

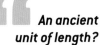

An ancient unit of length?

Carved in the stone of an outer corner of the chapel of Santa Lucia is a vertical rod some 1.5 metres long. In the 12th century, it was thought to be the standard for a destre, an ancient unit of length equivalent to eight palms, six feet, or two strides.

At the time, each kingdom used different measures, and in Barcelona the destre was 3,20 metres, about the same as Saint Lucy's yardstick, hence the belief that this was a standard unit of length. In fact, it is not quite eight palms long …

Some historians think that the carving indicates the water level before the chapel was built.

Another hypothesis is that it was just a whim of the architect.

WHAT UNITS OF LENGTH WERE USED IN SPAIN BEFORE THE METRE?

One of the most common units of length before the introduction of the metre was the legua (league), which measured the distance travelled in an hour by horse or man. This distance generally varied between 4 and 7 kilometres. In Spain the league was first defined as equal to 5,000 Castilian varas (yards), i.e. 4,190 metres, then towards the 16th century as 20,000 Castilian pies (feet), equivalent to 5,573 metres. The vara, equivalent to 33 pulgadas (inches - around 84 centimetres), was divided into 2 codos (cubits) or 4 palmos (palms). The braza (fathom), the distance across a man's outstretched arms, was a marine unit of length that eventually fell into disuse as it was inaccurate. The inch was measured by the breadth of a man's thumb at the base of the nail and the foot was the length of a man's foot. Other units of measurement used before the official adoption of the metre included the toesa cuadrada (area), the cordel (length), and the celemín and fanega (volumes of grain, etc.).

NEARBY

A LITTLE-KNOWN VIEWPOINT

13

Arxiu Històric de la Ciutat de Barcelona
Carrer de Santa Llúcia, 1 • Metro: Jaume I
• Tel: 93 318 1195
• Open Monday to Friday, 9.00–20.45; Saturday 9.00–13.00
• July and August Monday to Friday only, 9.00–13.00

The third floor of the Historic Archive of the City of Barcelona has bay windows overlooking Plaça de la Seu and Barcelona Cathedral. The view is spectacular from this select vantage point, known only to the lucky few. To reach it, you have to go up to the general reading room, the perfect place for those who like to immerse themselves in historical documents.

HIDDEN SYMBOLISM OF THE "DANCING EGG" ⑭ TRADITION

Cloister of Barcelona Cathedral
• Open Monday to Saturday 13.00–17.00, Sunday 14.00–17.00
Metro: Jaume I

> **Templars and masons in the cathedral**

During the Corpus Christi celebrations, a curious tradition known as *L'ou com balla* (The dancing egg) can be witnessed in the cloister of Barcelona Cathedral (Cathedral of the Holy Cross and Saint Eulalia). The idea is to balance an empty eggshell in the water jet of the fountain and watch it dance.

The egg holds a special place here in the cathedral because of the life of Saint Eulalia (see opposite), who kept geese. The goose is supposed to have laid an egg representing the beginning of Creation and the waters of life.

The goose was also a symbol of the builder monks who, following a way of life related to the secrets of architectural art based on sacred geometry, designed the cathedral.

In one of the Gothic cloisters live thirteen white geese to represent the age at which Eulalia, who kept geese near her home at Sarria, was martyred.

SAINT EULALIA: A MIRACULOUS VIRGIN, POPULARIZED BY THE TEMPLARS

Saint Eulalia, glorified in hymn III of Liber Peristephanon (Crowns of Martyrdom) by the Roman Christian poet Aurelius Prudencius (AD 348 to around 410), is one of the earliest surviving examples of hagiography from the Iberian peninsula. The poet relates that Eulalia lived near *Barcino* (modern Barcelona) in the 3rd or 4th centuries, at the time of the Emperor Diocletian (284–305) and Pope Marcellinus.

Refusing to renounce her Christian faith, Eulalia was tortured and finally crucified naked on an X-shaped cross. But her hair suddenly grew long and covered her to protect her modesty, while at the same time it began to snow. As she prayed to the Lord to bring her to His Kingdom, the executioners saw a white dove fly from her mouth.

The saint's relics were found in 878 by Bishop Frodoino, who solemnly carried them into the cathedral and laid them to rest in the crypt. The cathedral, which had been named for the Holy Cross (Sanctae Crucis) since 599, was then dedicated to Saint Eulalia too, and she became the city's patron saint.

The Templars were responsible for spreading the cult of Saint Eulalia as well as that of the Holy Cross, which still remains the heraldic emblem of the bishopric – a silver *croix pattée* (cross with feet) on a red background, similar to that of the ancient Order of the Knights Templar.

The cathedral's dedication is thus a medieval testimony to the direct presence of both Templars and builder monks, the early stonemasons.

STREETS IN THE BARRI GÒTIC NAMED AFTER GUILDS

 Daguería (cutlers), Agullers (needle makers), Cotoners (cotton weavers), Espaseria (gunsmiths), Mirallers (mirror dealers), Corders (rope makers), Fusteria (carpenters), Escudellers (shield makers) and Tapinería, where the shoemakers fashioned women's sandals from cork lined with leather and fabric, are just some of the street names in the Barcelona neighbourhood where the medieval guilds settled to ply their trades.

The guilds were family-based organizations or fraternal societies. The three most important of these guilds were the elois, the julians and the esteves, named after their respective patron saints Eloi (Eligius), Julian and Esteve (Stephen). It was not easy to be accepted by a guild, especially as membership was not hereditary.

It was gained by hard work: the apprentices had to respect a whole series of standards and demonstrate their skills in their chosen trade. The tests were difficult as the work had to be exemplary. For example, if a craftsman decided to use materials of inferior quality, the "examiners" who went round the workshops would force him to hang the faulty pieces from the shop door, and that would be the end of his reputation.

Although on a practical level the guilds existed to protect the interests of craftsmen, set prices, regulate relations between apprentice and master, and guarantee the quality of products, these powerful bodies maintained close links with the Church, negotiated special privileges with monarchs, and sent representatives to the Council of the Hundred.

In times of danger, the guilds were responsible for organizing the defence of the city. In other words, their influence was not limited to professional matters but had repercussions at every level of medieval Barcelona society.

Guild members did not only have premises in the same street, they also shared tools and the means of production. Moreover, the concentration of a group of craftsmen in the same area was practical for customers. Legend has it that a blind man wanting to know his whereabouts was guided by the smells emanating from the different workshops.

The bonds between the guilds and the Church were evident in the cults devoted to their respective patron saints. In Spain, Saints Abdon and Sennen were patrons of the gardeners' guild, Saint Peter of the fishermen, Saint John the Baptist of the tanners, while Saint Eulalia was both the official patron saint of the city and of masons. Doctors and barbers paid tribute to Saints Cosmas and Damian.

The blacksmiths were a special case, because the tools of all the others depended on them, as did weapons and chivalrous artefacts. They were protected by Saint Eloi.

These guilds existed for 600 years, until the mid-19th century when capitalism, and especially massive investment in industrial factories, spelled the end of the ancestral trades.

GUILD SYMBOLS

15

*Stoning
of the first
Christian martyr*

In the curved wall of the apse in the east wing of Barcelona Cathedral, almost opposite the Marès Museum, are two arresting sculptures. Both of them belong to Saint Stephen's guild, one of the three main medieval guilds, along with those of Saints Eloi and Julian.

They aimed to provide mutual assistance to their members, much like an insurance company today.

These two sculptures allude specifically to the saddlers' guild. The one on the left represents a saddle and a bit, symbols of the craftsmen who made and sold harness.

The second sculpture (below) is a crown of laurels encircling three stone spheres, which commemorates the stoning of Saint Stephen.

Saint Stephen's guild brings together various trades associated with

horsemanship and was very influential at the royal court in the 14th and 15th centuries.

The saddlers were highly respected and had their own chapel by the grand altar of the cathedral.

These symbols were carved in this part of the cathedral because it was closest to Carrer de la Frenería where the saddlers used to work.

SAINT STEPHEN, THE FIRST MARTYR

Known as the first Christian martyr, Saint Stephen was one of the seven deacons charged with helping the apostles.

He worked tirelessly to convert great numbers of Jews to the Christian faith. Accused of blasphemy against Moses and against God, he was stoned at the outskirts of Jerusalem.

There seems to be no particular reason why saddlers are associated with Saint Stephen. In fact, throughout its long history their fraternity had taken responsibility for a wide range of other trades, notably painters, lancers and embroiderers.

THE BREASTS OF SAINT AGATHA ⓰

Capella de Santa Ágata, Museu d'Història de la Ciutat
Plaça Reiál
• Metro: Catalunya, Urquinaona, Jaume I, Liceu
• Tel: 93 315 1111 • 1 October to 30 March: open Tuesday to Saturday,
10.00–14.00 and 16.00–19.00; 1 April to 30 September: open Tuesday
to Saturday, 10.00–20.00; and throughout the year open Sundays and
holidays, 10.00–15.00 • Admission: €6
• www.museuhistoria.bcn.cat

*Cruel
torment*

Built in 1302 by command of James II of Aragon, the Chapel of Saint Agatha is part of the Roman walls.

It is one of the most secluded religious edifices in the city, upstaged by the neighbouring buildings which include the City History Museum, where an archaeological site has been discovered underneath the buildings: 4,000 m^2 of Roman ruins, among which there is a 3rd-century winery.

In the chapel, the centerpiece is a painting of Saint Agatha holding up a tray on which are placed her own breasts. A little further on, the Condestable Altarpiece, a 15th-century work by Jaume Huguet, evokes the visit of the Magi. To the right of the altar, a small stairway leads to the 16th-century tower of King Martin I (the Humane) of Aragon.

Climbing these stairs, however, demands physical agility in addition to an interest in history.

SAINT AGATHA

Agatha, a pretty and devout daughter of a Sicilian noble family, was propositioned by the Roman senator Quintianus in the 3rd century, at a time when Christians were being persecuted by the Emperor Trajan. Faced by this Christian virgin's categorical refusal of his advances, he subjected her to the cruellest of tortures. First he sent her into a brothel, but miraculously, she emerged still a virgin. Then she was made to suffer a series of other torments, culminating in the mutilation of her breasts. Agatha was consoled by a vision of Saint Peter, who protected her from pain but not from death. In 250, just one year after her passing, Etna erupted and the islanders called on Saint Agatha to stop the flow of lava. Since that day, Agatha has been the patron saint of Catalonia and Sicily, as well as that of women with breast problems.

A BOMB IN THE HISTORY MUSEUM

On the night of 7 November 1893, the young anarchist Santiago Salvador went to the Liceu theatre to see a production of Rossini's opera William Tell, with two bombs concealed about his person. One of them killed twenty members of the audience in the orchestra pit. The other failed to detonate and is now on display at the City History Museum.

These circular metal bombs bear the mark of Felice Orsini (1819–1858), an Italian revolutionary who attempted to kill Napoleon III with a similar device, when he too was on his way to the opera.

SITE OF THE EXECUTIONER'S HOUSE   🗘

Plaça Reiál
• Metro: Jaume I

Sordid
details
of executions
under
the Inquisition ...

In Plaça Reiál, between the Chapel of Saint Agatha and Barcelona's City History Museum, a glass door gives onto a small room that was once the Hangman's House during the Inquisition. As the hangman could live neither in the city nor outside it, he was housed in the wall itself.

From the Middle Ages until almost the end of the 19th century, Plaça Reiál was indeed the final stop for those condemned to death, although the very last public execution in Barcelona (a wallet thief) took place on 15 June 1897 in Plaça Folchi i Torres.

The demanding job of executioner was one that nobody wanted. An executioner could no longer be touched, as his hands were supposed to have magical powers capable of destroying everything. For a while, it was even customary to leave a bag containing money and the instruments of execution in a corner of the square, brought in surreptitiously by an anonymous volunteer who turned up the next day to finish the accursed task. On some occasions nobody appeared, so butchers were summarily appointed as official executioners, skilled as they were in handling the tools. As a number of them committed suicide to avoid this duty, finally they were no longer forced into it and an official royal post was created, the holder of which enjoyed perks such as this small house near the Chapel of Saint Agatha. The executioner also kept the belongings of the deceased which he could then sell: shoes were very popular, for example, because if they were worn to enter a house it was supposed to be protected from evil spirits.

In 1492, when the peasant Joan de Canyamars stabbed King Ferdinand II of Aragon (Ferdinand the Catholic), his ordeal reached the heights of cruelty and sadism: he was paraded half-naked on a cart with the executioner. One of his hands was cut off in Plaça del Blat and the other at El Born; then in Plaça Sant Jaume they cut off his nose, gouged out an eye and hacked off a leg while he bled to death in front of the crowds. In Plaça Santa Ana, his other eye was taken out and the remaining leg cut off, and finally what remained of the unfortunate's body was quartered and taken outside the city to burn at Canyet.

As the prison also used to be in Plaça Reiál, when someone was about to be executed a sign listing his crimes was hung on his chest. Sometimes he was also made to wear a red belt to which was attached the equipment he had used to commit the crime. Having paraded the condemned man through the city streets to be seen and booed by all and sundry, the procession returned to the

square, where the scaffold was ready and waiting. The judges were careful to keep the condemned alive to endure the pain of punishment, which is why they were always accompanied by a surgeon.

Accomplices to any crime were also flogged and forced to watch the hanging or ordeal by fire. Nobles and clergy were garroted, sometimes had their throats cut or were beheaded, as were the military (the firing squad was only introduced later). Homosexuals and heretics were burned alive, and plebs were hanged. Women who had committed some crime (except cases of heresy, for which they were burned) were exposed naked on a donkey and paraded through the city so people could insult them. For heretics, the Inquisition used the so-called "judgment of God according to the *aguadija*": a huge set of scales was brought to Plaça Reiál, where a Bible was placed in one of its pans and the suspected heretic in the other. If the person weighed less than the Bible, their innocence was proven.

At No. 1 Plaça del Pi, the sign of the Arxiconfraria de la Puríssima Sang de Nostre Senyor Jesucrist (Arch-Confraternity of the Most Pure Blood of Our Lord Jesus Christ) recalls the existence of this brotherhood which, in the 14th century, brought spiritual succour to the condemned of Plaça Reiál.

EROTIC SCULPTURES AT PALAU DEL LLOCTINENT

Plaça Reiál
• Metro: Catalunya

Self-indulgent angels

Charles V's palace was built under the supervision of Antoni Carbonell following a decree by the Monzón (Aragon) Parliament in 1547. From 1863 to 1993 it housed the Archives of the Crown of Aragon. Although Lluís Domènech was responsible for modernizing the facilities at Palau del Lloctinent in 1987, a major restoration was carried out between 2002 and 2006.

This building, originally the residence of the Spanish *lloctinent* (viceroy) of Catalonia, was completed in 1558. So that Charles V could avoid mixing with the common people, a passage led firstly to the royal gallery of the cathedral via a bridge over Carrer dels Comtes (from the street you can still see part of the bridge), and secondly to the Royal Chapel of Saint Agatha in Plaça Reiál. Curiously, during the 1987 restoration work a gargoyle resembling the

"Dragon Khan" attraction of PortAventura amusement park was placed where it can be seen from the courtyard.

As he was not on good terms with Jaume Cassador, the Bishop of Barcelona, Charles V had erotic sculptures set around the palace to scandalize the canons as they approached what was then the main entrance to Barcelona Cathedral in Carrer dels Comtes – Sant Iu's door.

One of them shows a *putto* (nude and chubby child) inserting a bellows into the anus of another, who seems to be taking pleasure in it. On this same façade, another *putto* is fellating the enormous phallus of a monster.

STREETLAMPS IN PLAÇA REIÁL

Plaça Reiál
• Metro: Jaume I

I n the square beside the History Museum are replicas of three medieval streetlamps (there are another two in Plaça de Santa María del Mar).

Let there be light ...

These lamps used resin as fuel, which ignited readily, took a long time to burn and gave off a pleasant smell.

That was very important at the time and served the same purpose as incense in church – neutralizing the smell that filled any space where a great number of pilgrims were gathered, in the days before deodorants and shampoos.

Around 1725, this type of oil lamp was still being used in Barcelona. A century later, on the evening of 24 June 1826, the feast day of Saint John, gas lamps lit up for the first time the building that houses the former Barcelona stock exchange (Llotja).

From 1842 onwards, the same system began to be used for lighting La Rambla and other streets and squares.

The following year, the Frenchman Charles Lebon planned the construction of the first gas production plant, the Sociedad Catalana para el Alumbrado por Gas (Catalan Gaslight Company), which provided lighting on an industrial scale, especially in the developing new factories.

Electric light was not generally available in Barcelona before 1904, although the beginnings of the electrical industry go back to 1873. In that year, the Barcelona optician and physician Tomás Dalmau and the engineer Narciso Xifrá inaugurated the first electricity generating plant.

The system worked with four gas-powered motors that drove machines each producing 200 voltamperes.

These supplied electricity to various premises in the city. 1888 saw the installation of the first electric lampposts, which were to coexist with the gas lamps until the mid-20th century.

In the same square, between the Chapel of Saint Agatha and the City History Museum, a glass door reveals a small room where the Inquisition hangman used to live (see page 46).

THE ANGEL OF PLAÇA DEL ÁNGEL ⓴

Plaça del Ángel, 2
• Metro: Jaume I

Saint Eulalia's miracle

At No. 2 Plaça del Ángel stands a curious bronze figure, thought to be an angel. The left arm of this androgynous figure, wingless and bearing a cross on its forehead, is pointing with an outstretched finger to a spot said to be the site of a miracle – the archway in Baixada de la Llibretería, where there used to be a portrait of Saint Eulalia, patron of the city of Barcelona.

Legend has it that in 879 the mortal remains of the saint were being transferred from Santa María del Mar church to the cathedral. Along the way, someone stole one of Eulalia's fingers and, until it was restored, no human force could move the rest of her body.

The sculpture in Plaça del Ángel is a replica.

The original, which dates from 1618, is in the City History Museum. The portrait of Saint Eulalia disappeared at the end of the 19th century.

NEARBY

THE OLDEST SHOP IN TOWN ⓴

Baixada Llibreteria, 7
• Tel: 93 315 2606
• Open Monday to Friday, 9.00–13.30; Saturday, 16.00–19.30

A short distance from Plaça Sant Jaume can be found Cerería Subirá, the oldest shop in Barcelona.

Although the shop has been open since 1761, it was renovated in 1847, and the site has been owned by just two families over the 250 years of its existence. Such is its reputation that the churches of Barcelona now buy half its total output. The other half goes to customers who like decorative candles, which range from Disney characters to more sophisticated creations.

Things have not always gone smoothly for Cerería Subirá but it has coped with various setbacks. After the Civil War, not many people could see any beauty in a candle – far from seeming romantic or intimate, candlelight was instead a reminder of a time of restrictions and suffering.

REMAINS OF A ROMAN TEMPLE ㉒

Carrer del Paradís, 10
• Metro: Catalunya
• Free entry at the Centre Excursionista de Catalunya, usually closed in winter

> **Probably not the Temple of Augustus**

In Carrer del Paradís, at the entrance to the Centre Excursionista de Catalunya courtyard, there is a distinctive millstone fixed to the ground and a plaque marking the highest point of the Old City of Barcelona (Mont Tàber, 16.9 metres above sea level). Here lie the ruins of an ancient temple which was part of the Roman forum, now Plaça de Sant Jaume (today much reduced in size).

Of the four remaining columns in the upper right-hand corner of the temple, one is not original but was brought here from Plaça Reiál. Part of the architrave has also been preserved although it was integrated in a later construction. The temple was 35 metres long and 17.5 metres wide, with the perimeter columns set on a podium.

These columns, which are the best-preserved Roman ruins in Barcelona, are commonly believed to be the remains of the temple dedicated to the Emperor Augustus Caesar. In 2007, however, a team carrying out excavations over 35 m² in the vicinity of the main access to the nave of Tarragona Cathedral found the foundations and steps of a temple. Experts believe that this is the authentic site of the temple that was dedicated to Augustus in the region.

According to the archaeologists responsible for the dig: "We cannot categorically state that this temple was dedicated to the Emperor Augustus, but a series of finds leads us to think it highly probable. We have been able to show that this was an octostyle temple (eight columns on the façade) at the centre of an arcaded gallery resembling the architecture of the Forum of Augustus at Rome, dominated by the Temple of Mars Ultor (Mars the Avenger)."

Tarragona (Tarraco) was also the capital of Roman Hispania. It was therefore logical that a temple should be built to the glory of Augustus at Tarragona, where he had spent some time during his reign, rather than at Barcelona.

ROMAN BARCELONA

In AD 15, Barcelona was known as Colonia Augusta Faventia Paterna Barcino, or simply Barcino.

The existing city was built over the remains of the Roman one, of which several vestiges can still be seen, the most spectacular of which must be the 3rd-century Roman ramparts.

The brick and mortar walls were almost 2 metres thick with a perimeter of 1,250 metres. The 10 hectare area of enclosed ground was coffin-shaped with four entrances (part of one of the gates is in Carrer de Regomir). The ramparts that can be seen today were constructed on the outer face of the earlier ones, to a height of 8 metres. They were equipped with sixty-six towers.

In the Middle Ages, the ancient fortified walls became too confining for the prosperous and expanding city, so King James I of Aragon ordered new walls built, an endeavour that took over a century.

These new walls, which enclosed the principal neighbourhoods of the time, covered an area ten times the size of the Roman city and corresponded to the area now known as the Barri Gòtic.

For more information on the vestiges of Roman Barcelona, see following double-page spread.

VESTIGES OF ROMAN BARCELONA

1 Roman necropolis – Plaça de la Vila de Madrid
The tombs have an opening through which relatives could leave flowers and food for their dead. Not far away, a small museum displays relics found in the tombs, such as miniature glass bottles where the tears shed during funerals were collected and coins with which the deceased paid Hades' ferryman to cross the Styx to the underworld.

2 Roman aqueduct – Plaça del Vuit de Març
In 1988, the demolition of a former parking lot led to the chance discovery of the Roman aqueduct. It had been preserved and used as a dividing wall and corresponds to a small section of four arches some 20 metres long and 4.10 metres high.

3 Porta Decumana – Plaça Nova
This square was the northern entrance to the Roman city. The two towers and the Roman wall date from the 1st and 4th centuries BC, although the path leading inside was built in 1358. In the left tower are the ruins of the aqueduct that brought water to the city along two courses, one from the Collserola mountain range and the other from the Besòs River.

4 Roman wall – between Plaça de Ramon Berenguer el Gran and Plaça d'Emili Vilanova
From Plaça Ramon de Berenguer el Gran two types of wall can be seen, Roman (below – 1st century BC, fortified in the 4th century) and medieval (above). This leads to Plaça d'Emili Vilanova, where there is another section of ruins (tombstones, pedestals and sculptures used to strengthen the wall).

5 Temple of Augustus – Carrer del Paradís, 10. See p. 54.

6 Roman gate leading to the sea – Centre Cívic Pati Llimona – Carrer del Regomir, 3
The southern gate was the main entrance to the Roman city that led directly to the sea. In 1984, the remains of the gate were discovered.

7 Museu d'Història de la Ciutat – Plaça Reiál
During the restoration of Barcelona's City History Museum in 1931, extensive Roman ruins were discovered underneath Plaça Reiál. Most of these ruins correspond to agricultural and craft workshops for washing and dyeing, the production of wine and salted fish.

8 Defensive tower – Plaça dels Traginers
Part of the ruins of the Roman wall with its defensive tower dating from the 4th century.

9 Casal de Gent Gran Pati Llimona – Carrer del Correu Vell, 5
Within this public facility for senior citizens is an important section of the Roman wall.

10 Demolished wall – Carrer del Call, 7
Building dating from the 15th century, built on top of the Roman wall. At one place, the ruins of a demolished section of the wall can be seen.

11 Two Roman towers – Carrer d'Avinyó, 19
Inside a restaurant, in the lower section, are the walls of two Roman towers.

12 Centre Sinia – Carrer dels Banys Nous, 16
Hidden within this centre for disabled people is part of the Roman wall.

13 Domus – Carrer de la Fruita, 2
Ruins of a Roman house dating from the 4th century and of a *tabernae* (commercial building).

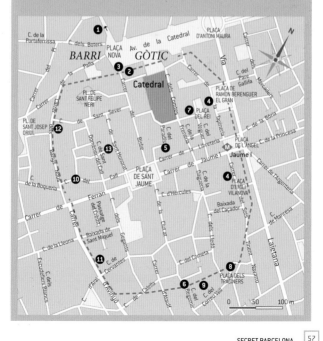

MASONIC DEATH'S HEAD   ㉓

Calle del Bisbe
• Metro Catalunya

> *Symbolism*
> *of Gaudí's disciple*
> *Joan Rubió*

Known for being one of the most prolific Modernist architects, Joan Rubió i Bellver left a legacy that is curious to say the least. A disciple of Antoni Gaudí, with whom he worked until 1905, he collaborated on projects such as the Sagrada Família (Basilica and Expiatory Church of the Holy Family), Casa Batlló, Casa Calvet, the castle known as Torre Bellesguard, Park Güell, the restoration of the Cathedral of Mallorca and the Colònia Güell (factory town), where he built several houses but never worked directly on the Güell Crypt.

Joan Rubió carried out restoration work at Carrer del Bisbe along with another architect, Jeroni Martorell, who was responsible for the other side of Casa dels Canonges. Under the Arzobispo bridge, also the work of Joan Rubió, which links Casa dels Canonges with the Palau de la Generalitat, a skull with a dagger implanted in it serves as a keystone. Nearby an acacia and some royal symbols are featured.

According to the city's ancient legends, if you cross the bridge walking backwards, you can make a wish. This myth is born of the notion that Barcelona's citizens don't see what's in front of them: two of the elements found in Masonic reflections.

The skull and dagger symbolize initiatory death, understood as an allegorical death – when the allegorical man dies, all the conditioning, limitations and prejudices of the ordinary mortal, slave to the obvious, transient and continuing, die with him. Thus the opportunity arises to regain consciousness in eternity along with true liberation.

If anyone doubts that this skull and dagger are Masonic symbols, note that nearby walls bear other symbols of Freemasonry, such as the ibis, the letter *tau* and the white glove.

ACACIA: MASONIC SYMBOL OF IMMORTALITY

The presence of the acacia branch is also very significant: this is the plant selected by Universal Freemasonry to designate the Master Mason, Masonic initiation and immortality, attained through the state of innocence and purity that the ancient Dorians and Ionians named *akákia*. The word "acacia" is derived from the Greek *aké*, which means tip or extremely sharp, a sense that was later given to *lanké* (spear). The ancient description of this thorny plant was *akantha*, meaning plant with spines: acanthus, acacia, hence *akákia*. These thorns represent the painful trials that the initiate faces and must overcome on the path that will lead to the Perfect Master's degree.

BLACK MADONNA AT THE CHURCH OF SANTS JUST I PASTOR

Riera de Sant Just, s/n
- Metro: Jaume I
- Tel: 93 301 7433
- Open Monday to Saturday 11.00–14.00 and 17.30–21.00 (20.00 Tuesday); Sunday 10.00–13.00

Where is the real Moreneta?

On the altar of the church of Saints Justus and Pastor is a statue thought to be a replica of the Black Madonna, the Virgin of Montserrat, patron saint of Catalonia since 1881 by decree of Pope Leo XIII.

Although legend has it that the statue was found by shepherds on a Saturday afternoon in 880, it is actually a Romanesque sculpture dating from the 12th century, as claimed by the Benedictine monks. The poplar-wood Moreneta ("Little Black Lady") is 95 centimetres tall and holds the Infant Jesus to her breast.

The child has a pine cone in his hand, and although many people have seen this as an esoteric symbol, the cone had simply become a sign of hospitality in Europe during the Italian Renaissance. Innkeepers later adopted the habit of spreading pine cones around. As time passed, someone must have decided to replace the book Jesus held in his hand with this pine cone.

In the 17th century, during the night of the Holy Trinity, the Sunday after Pentecost, fifty days after Easter Sunday, the Black Madonna was damaged after a fire in the niche where she stood. After the Napoleonic Wars (1799–1802), while Napoleon's troops plundered the Black Madonna's jewellery and left the statue exposed to the elements for weeks, a monk from the Benedictine Abbey of Montserrat wrote in 1812: "For reasons that we all know, the face and hands of Our Lady were retouched, which showed that the colour of the statue was uniform, and the face of the child was therefore painted in light brown, as it was before." This is mentioned in the Montserrat archives, *bolsa* 7/74ᵃ. This parchment also mentions that the sphere in her hand was painted gold.

The Black Madonna was restored by Joan Cunyás Sala and turned up on 12 June 1824 at the monastery of Montserrat. The child figure was replaced, as were the pine cone, arms and hands, with newer versions.

In 1931 the sculpture was removed from its niche to keep it out of the hands of Franco supporters. Only three monks knew where it was. On 26 February 1939 La Moreneta returned to Montserrat, without anyone knowing from whence it came.

During the 2001 restoration an X-ray revealed that there is no hole in the upper part of the globe carried by the Virgin. This is important because the Black Madonna of Sant Just i Pastor is the only official replica that has a hole at the top. However, chromolithographs made at the time when Leo XIII

proclaimed the Virgin as patron saint of Catalonia showed that the Black Madonna, who appeared on all these images, had a hole where a lily or palm was placed. You can see an example on the ceiling of a salon in the Palau de la Generalitat of Catalonia.

Bearing in mind that there is a document in the church of Sants Just i Pastor, signed by the Benedictines, stating that they returned the wooden sculpture to the basilica in 1931, we can conclude that the Black Madonna was perhaps never restored to Montserrat, and the figure now revered on the sacred mountain is nothing but a replica.

Moreover, the Black Madonna of Sants Just i Pastor contains traces of brown paint and a burnished sphere, not golden, as mentioned in *bolsa* 7/74[a] of the monastery archives.

It is said that the Virgin is black because the original paint contained lead, which reacted with sulphur oxide in the air and darkened the image. Another story is that a macroscopic view of the last restoration in 2001 reveals, on the face and neck, an older layer of greenish-brown paint and another layer of newer black paint. But there are no traces of insect damage, although the Black Madonna was exposed to the elements during the Napoleonic wars. Finally, the original colours are missing from the body of the statue and even the Benedictine monks recognize that this is too recent a restoration.

THE THIRTEEN EMBLEMS OF THE VAULT OF SANTS JUST I PASTOR CHURCH ㉕

Riera de Sant Just, s/n
- Metro: Jaume I
- Tel: 93 301 7433
- Open Monday to Saturday 11.00–14.00 and 17.30–21.00 (20.00 Tuesday); Sunday 10.00–13.00

> *Mysterious emblems form the constellation of Gemini ...*

The basilica church of Saints Justus and Pastor bears the names of the two brothers venerated as Christian martyrs who were born at Tielmes near Madrid and executed aged 13 and 9 in AD 304 at Alcalá de Henares (where they are buried) by order of the consul Dacien, apparently authorized by the Roman Emperor Diocletian.

It seems, however, that these two saints never actually existed and that the Roman Catholic Church, wanting to put an end to paganism by incorporating ancient beliefs, invented the characters as a substitute for the cult of Castor and Pollux.

The builders of the basilica must have been aware of this story because on the ceiling you can see that the thirteen emblems near the keystone arches of the vault, taken together, form the constellation Gemini, which in mythology is associated with Castor and Pollux (see below).

CASTOR AND POLLUX, TWO BROTHERS, ONE MORTAL, THE OTHER DEMIGOD, UNITED IN THE CONSTELLATION OF THE TWINS

In Greek mythology, Castor and Pollux were the sons of Leda and the brothers of Helen of Troy. Leda, wife of Tyndareus, was also united with Zeus, who had transformed himself into a swan to seduce her. She was thought to have laid two eggs: the one from the union with Zeus contained Pollux and Helen (who were therefore demigods) and the other from the union with Tyndareus contained Castor and his sister Clytemnestra, who were mere mortals.

As the twins were inseparable, when Castor died Pollux refused immortality so as not to be separated from his brother. It was decided that the two brothers would spend half the year together in the underworld, and the other half in heaven, where Zeus placed the pair in the constellation of Gemini.

WHY IS HERCULES STREET RIGHT NEXT TO SANTS JUST I PASTOR?

Castor and Pollux were among those who took part in the expedition of the Argonauts in search of the Golden Fleece and fought Theseus to recover their sister Helen from him.

As Hercules had accompanied Jason in his quest for the Golden Fleece, as well as Castor and Pollux, one of Barcelona's streets next to the basilica now bears his name.

It is also said that Hercules went to Barcelona in search of the twins and named the city Barcanova, a word derived from "Barca" (a particularly important family in the Punic Wars between Rome and Carthage) and "Nova" (new), an etymology similar to that of Carthage (Carthago Nova).

THE FIGURE OF GEMINI: SPIRITUAL INITIATES, FOUNDERS OF CITIES AND CIVILIZATIONS?

Castor and Pollux and Saints Justus and Pastor are also reminders of the Roman figures of Romulus and Remus, who were suckled by the wolf Italica, a legend dealing with the transmission of ancestral wisdom (represented by the twins fed by the wolf, an animal held to be esoteric and secretive). Note that in Christian tradition, Jesus also addresses John as his brother at Calvary.

Thus these sets of twins, initiated to the divine wisdom, will through their joint efforts be able to access the higher mysteries of the sacred tradition. Hence they will return in possession of a supernatural power, able to act directly on matter and bring forth the greatest prodigies defined by the people as miraculous divine interventions.

They are indeed always represented as achievers of superhuman feats, heroic navigators who act as guides, initiators of civilizations and founders of cities: Romulus and Remus founded Rome; Castor and Pollux were there at the beginning of the Hellenic civilization; the Celtic dioscuri Momoros and Atepomaros founded Lugdunum (Lyon); and Justus and Pastor, although they died young, are behind the greatness of the Roman settlements of Complutum (Alcalá de Henares), as well as Compludo (Bierzo), all founded under their protection.

PORTRAIT OF FRUCTUÓS CANONGE 26

Carrer del Pas de l'Ensenyança, 1
• Metro: Jaume I

A
celebrated
shoeshine boy

Fructuós Canonge i Francesch (1824–90), nicknamed the Gran Canonge or Catalan Merlin, is one of the most striking characters in the history of Barcelona. His family escaped from the poverty of Montbrió del Camp (Tarragona) and moved to Barcelona seven years after his birth. After trying various jobs, he established a shoeshine stall in Plaça Reiál whose sign is still in the porch, near the Colón brewery.

After serving a prison sentence in Cuba for failing to comply with a curfew during the 1856 uprisings, he returned to Barcelona where his sense of humour, eccentricities (he ate shoe-polish to show that it was good quality) and illusionist's tricks (he made cigarettes appear behind the ears of bystanders and broke eggs on the steps to extract gold coins from them) made him famous.

After making his debut in 1858 at the Teatre dels Camps Elisis on Passeig de Gràcia, he became one of the best-known magicians of his time and travelled throughout Spain, France and South America. Doors were opened to him in the top theatres and palaces, and he even performed for Queen Isabella II,

Fructuoso Canonge

Prince Amedeo of Savoy and King Alfonso XII. He received various titles and decorations, including the Cross of the Order of Isabella the Catholic and the Cross of the Order of Charles III, which he always wore proudly on his chest. Between the years 1860 and 1870, he was also the leading light of Barcelona Carnival. Although he earned plenty of money as a magician, he died in poverty at the age of 66 at his home in Carrer de la Canuda.

In 2003, Barcelona City Council restored the mural dedicated to him in Pas de l'Ensenyança, where he is shown pulling a rabbit out of his hat.

RUINS OF THE SINAGOGA MAYOR

27

Carrer de Marlet, 5
• Metro: Liceu
• Tel: 93 317 0790 • Open Monday to Saturday, 11.00–14.30 and
16.00–19.30
• Admission: €2
• www.calldebarcelona.org

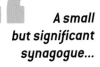

*A small
but significant
synagogue...*

Symbolic of El Call, the Jewish quarter within the Barri Gòtic, is the Main Synagogue dating from the 1st century. Part of the original building remains, facing towards Jerusalem. Despite its name, the Main Synagogue is tiny – only 60 m², as synagogues were not allowed to exceed 80 m² at the time. There is an exhibition in the synagogue that reconstitutes the ancient Call, overlooking the Roman forum. Also on display are a number of relics, notably the pewter plates used during Passover by Eastern European Jewish families, and a menorah by Majorcan artist Ferrán Aguiló.

The Main Synagogue had not been used for worship since 1391.

Now restored, it is currently run by a group of conservationists (Associació Call de Barcelona) and hosts Jewish celebrations such as bar mitzvahs and marriages.

NEARBY

THE PLAQUE OF SAMUEL ASARDI

28

Outside the synagogue is a plaque inscribed in Hebrew. It was discovered in 1820 and dates from the 12th century. The text, "that his name shall never be extinguished, that his light shall burn eternally," was written in tribute to Samuel Asardi, a rabbi who in 1200 gifted a house to charity. As the original plaque was being persistently vandalized it has been transferred to the City History Museum. The one you can see at Carrer de Marlet is a replica.

EL CALL

The word "Call", which comes from the Hebrew qahal (assembly), designates the Jewish neighbourhoods of Catalan towns. Barcelona's Jewish quarter extends from the gates of Castell Nou and the Episcopal Palace, which used to form part of the Roman ramparts, between Arc de Sant Ramón, Call, Bisbe and Sant Sever streets. In the mid-12th century it stretched as far as the present church of Sant Jaume, in the area known as Call Menor (Little Call). The influence of the Jews of El Call in Barcelona reached its height in the 12th–14th centuries, due to their prosperous businesses as much their role as money-lenders to James I of Aragon and his successors. In 1391, after an anti-Semitic pogrom throughout Spain left numerous victims, the gates of the Jewish ghetto in Barcelona were torn down. Of the survivors, many were forced to flee and others converted to Christianity. In 1424, all of the remaining Jews were expelled from El Call, and in 1492, from Barcelona and the whole of Spain.

JEWISH MENORAH IN THE CHURCH OF SANT JAUME 🔞

Carrer de Ferrán, 28
• Metro: Liceu
• santjaume102@arqbcn.org
• Open daily, 10.00–14.00 and 17.00–20.00
• Adoration of the Blessed Sacrament: Tuesday, Wednesday and Thursday 20.30, Saturday 21.00, Sunday 18.00
• Compline: Tuesday, Wednesday and Thursday 21.30

A former Jewish synagogue

For centuries, the city's oldest synagogue occupied the site where the church of Sant Jaume now stands, in Carrer de Ferrán, a street in the *"antiguo Call Menor"* (old Little Call). This district was built outside the city walls when the traditional Jewish quarter expanded, demolishing the medieval walls in the process.

Following the attack that tore apart the Jewish quarter on 5 August 1391, the feast of Saint Dominic, the building was handed over to nuns who set up a convent there. It passed to the Trinitarians from 1522 until 1529 and in 1619 the Consell de Cent (Council of the Hundred) gave permission for the

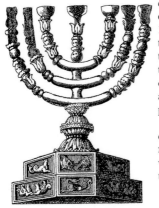

church to be enlarged, thus blocking off the alleyway behind the apse. In 1835 thirty-five monks were living there as well as some novices. When the religious community dispersed, the cloister and other buildings were destroyed, while the church remained and became the seat of the present parish of Sant Jaume.

As a tribute to the building's Jewish origins, inside is a menorah (Hebrew הַרוֹנמ), the oil lamp or candelabrum with seven branches that forms one of the ritual elements of Judaism.

OTHER HEBREW TRACES IN THE OLD JEWISH QUARTER

In the two little streets called Volta del Remei and Arco de Santa Eulalia you can still see not only Hebrew engravings, but the holes in the walls where the Jews placed their prayers.

The menorah represents the burning bush that Moses saw on Mount Sinai (Exodus 3).

THE FOUNTAIN OF THE KING'S HERBORIUM ③⓪

Carrer del Vidre, 1
• Metro: Liceu
• Tel: 93 318 0512
• Open Tuesday to Friday, 16.00–20.00; Saturday, 10.00–20.00

Leeches for apoplexy ...

Founded in 1823, the king's herborium has retained (with a few Gothic touches) its décor from the era of Queen Isabella II, designed by the renowned scenographer Francesc Soler i Rovirosa.

On the ground floor of the shop are sea chests from a late 18th-century ship and, on the ceiling, frescoes that are over 100 years old.

Also of note is a sculpture by Fausto Baratta Rossi commemorating Carl Von Linné (Linnaeus), the Swedish botanist who perfected the classification and nomenclature of plants.

The sculpture incorporates a small fountain for keeping leeches, those little creatures that were once used to lower patients' blood pressure if they were likely to have a stroke. It is commonly thought that the bust on top of the leech fountain is that of Charles III, because of the type of wig he is wearing, but it is in fact Linnaeus.

Until 1857, when Isabella II granted the herborium the title "purveyor to the royal household," it was known as La Linneana after the botanist.

Currently, the shop sells 200 types of medicinal plant, ranging from the classic chamomile for daily infusions to mauve for treating respiratory problems, as well as ginkgo biloba for improving the flow of blood to the brain. Other than medicinal plants and herbs, it offers premium quality products such as olive oil, saffron, and honey.

NEARBY

RENT A WORK OF ART ③①
Crea 21 Galerie d'Art
Passatge de la Pau, 14
• Metro: Drassanes
• Tel: 93 317 5851
• Open Monday to Friday, 11.00–20.00
• www.crea21.net

If you want to impress friends with remarkable works of art, Crea 21 is the place for you. This exhibition space and art salesroom offers a large catalogue of works for hire, for businesses or for private homes. You can also change your pieces of art as often as you desire.

Other than art for rent, Crea 21 offers a personalized gift service. If you like the work of any particular artist, they can make a piece to order.

HARE KRISHNA TEMPLE

32

Carrer de N'Aglá, 14, mezzanine B
• Metro: Liceu
• Tel: 93 302 5194
• Open daily
• Menu: €7

After lunch, you can visit the temple ...

The Hare Krishna temple opens its dining room everyday to anyone who accepts its conditions: there is no set menu, you eat whatever is on offer that day, but it is strictly vegetarian, consisting of salad, soup, main dish, dessert, and water. No other drinks are available.

The main entrance is very discreet – there is no notice board, just a doorplate. Inside, the ambience is festive, with incense floating in the air and joyful background music. The dining room has a small terrace and large windows that bathe the place in light.

After lunch, you can visit the temple: a very spacious hall that you must enter barefoot, dominated by a life-size statue of the founder of the world Hare Krishna movement, A.C. Bhaktivedanta Swami Prabhupada. Both the meal and tour are informal, as are the Sunday open days, aimed at attracting new members.

WHO ARE HARE KRISHNA?

The group known as the International Society for Krishna Consciousness (ISKCON) preaches a faith based on traditional Vaishnava Hinduism, practises bhakti yoga, and worships the god Krishna (literally "principal deity"). Inspired by the teaching of the Bengali saint Caitanya Mahaprabhu (1486–1533), the name of the movement comes from the words of the maja mantra (main prayer) chanted by its adherents.

In 1966, Abhay Charanaravinda Bhaktivedanta Swami Prabhupada took his teachings to New York, where he set up a base from which to promote and sell his books in airports and on the street, rapidly increasing the number of followers.

Hare Krishna devotees routinely live apart from their families, believe in reincarnation, and refuse to touch alcohol, tea, cigarettes, meat, or eggs. They do not gamble and sex is for reproductive purposes only.

GAUDÍ'S STREETLAMPS

Plaça Reiál, s/n
• Metro: Drassanes
Pla de Palau, s/n
• Metro: Barceloneta

> *Of the six lamps designed by Gaudí, only four remain*

The *fanals* (lamps) in Barcelona's Plaça Reiál are quite amazing and worth a closer look. They were designed by the Modernist architect Antoni Gaudí i Cornet (1852–1926) as one of his first commissions in 1879. This was a month before he graduated as an architect and started work as a designer with Josep Fontserè, a Freemason like himself (see p. 189 and 193), which probably explains why he was given this commission.

Gaudí designed two different types of lamp, one with three and the other with six branches. Two of these lamps, with a stone base and bronze and wrought-iron posts, grace Plaça Reiál. However, given their high price (3,500 pesetas at the time), Barcelona City Council wanted the others to be cheaper. Gaudí simplified the design so that each lamp would cost no more than 1,500 pesetas, but after that he no longer wanted to work for the council, despite its insistence on trying to appoint him as official architect. Minimalism had no place in his extravagant style.

The decoration of the upper section of the Plaça Reiál streetlamps is particularly striking, featuring the Roman god Mercury with winged helmet and two snakes coiled around the centre post. These lamps were installed in September 1879.

The location of the lamps between the Masonic lodges of General Madoz and Ildefons Cerdà is an interesting detail, hinting at the fact that Gaudí was probably a Freemason.

In 1890 the three-branched lamps, also in pairs, were installed in front of the municipal buildings in Pla de Palau.

Of Gaudí's six lamps, the two originally in Paseo Juan de Borbón in the Barceloneta neighbourhood are missing. Nobody knows where they are now. The official explanation is that they are "lost".

TRACES OF PROSTITUTES

34

La Rambla, 22 and 24

Streetwalkers' legacy

The marks worn in the pavement in front of Nos. 22 and 24 La Rambla have a certain historical significance, completely unknown even to most local residents. They were made by the prostitutes who, over a number of years, paced backwards and forwards on this spot, waiting for clients. Over time, the pressure of their heels wore down the marble and left these indentations for posterity. In 1956, prostitution was banned by the authorities and brothels were closed. The girls were thus forced to seek out their clients on the street and especially, as was the case at Nos. 22 and 24, at the doors of small hotels.

For many years, the bottom end of La Rambla near the port was a favourite place for buying and selling sex, but the practice was stamped out in the run-up to the 1992 Olympic Games. The municipality and the Friends of the Ramblas association invested millions of pesetas to renovate the area.

LOVE HOTELS

Offering rooms by the hour, love hotels, like those in Japan, are meant for couples. Many of those in Barcelona are designer-built and they are all decorated to satisfy their clients' fantasies: round beds, ceiling mirror, pornographic TV channels, jacuzzis.

La França is one of the biggest and best known, with over seventy luxurious rooms, and it provides private parking, even going so far as covering vehicle license plates to ensure complete discretion.

In the very heart of Barcelona, in El Raval area, La Paloma is a modern hotel for a younger age-group, offering more reasonable tarifs. The Regàs hotel in Gràcia runs a similar service.

At these three hotels, and generally speaking, at all the love hotels, once you have left the room you cannot return, and there is no need to book in advance. Homosexual couples are welcome, but three in a bed is strictly taboo.

La França - La França Xica, 40; Tel: 93 423 1416; www.lafransa.com
Regàs - Regàs, 10–12; Tel: 93 238 0092; www.hregas.com
La Paloma - La Paloma, 24–26; Tel: 93 412 4381; www.hlapaloma.com

CATALAN STATUES ON THE COLUMBUS MONUMENT

㉟

Plaça del Portal de la Pau
• Metro: Drassanes
• Mirador: open 8.30–20.30
• Closed 25 December and 1 January
• Admission: €4

Was Christopher Columbus Catalan?

Many nationalities have been attributed to Christopher Columbus (1451–1506): Genoese, Corsican, Portuguese, Spanish, Catalan, Majorcan, Galician or a native of Ibiza, among others. Those who favour Catalan origins believe his real name was "Colom" and state that his writings contain many typically Catalan twists and turns such as *a todo arreo* (on all sides), *todo de un golpe* (suddenly) or *setcentas* (seven hundred). This is inconclusive evidence, however, and supporters of other nationalities base their convictions on equally if not more compelling arguments. As Columbus never left any known writings about his place of birth or origins, it might be more accurate to say that he came from everywhere. He knew Hebrew, Latin, Castilian Spanish, Catalan and Portuguese; he sailed the seas of the North, the Mediterranean, the Atlantic and the Caribbean; and he served kings far and wide and lived among people of very different cultures and languages.

For the 1888 Universal Exposition, Barcelona erected the world's tallest monument to Columbus (his statue tops a 60-metre column). The work of architect Gaietà Buigas and sculptor Rafael Atché, the Columbus monument is a favourite target for tourist cameras. Few people, however, notice that the figures around the stone base recall the explorer's close links with Catalonia. They feature, for example, Lluís de Santàngel, the Valencian *converso* (converted Jew) settled in Barcelona who helped to finance the 1492 voyage, holding a small chest; and Jaume Ferrer de Blanes, a Catalan astronomer who advised Columbus before he left, pointing to a globe; there is also Pere de Margarit, military leader of the second voyage, represented with helmet and armour; and finally, Brother Bernat de Boïl, a monk from Montserrat who sailed on the second expedition.

The submissive demeanour of the Native Americans accompanying Bernat de Boïl and Pere de Margarit is only too obvious.

REMINDERS OF THE KNIGHTS TEMPLAR IN BARCELONA

The Barcelona commandery of the Ancient Order of the Poor Knights of Christ and of the Temple of Solomon, commonly referred to as the Templars, was one of the richest and most important in Spain. One of the reasons for this was control over the important seaport, which was used by the Catalan Templars notably in their relations with the Holy Land and other Mediterranean regions.

Some architectural traces still survive of the presence of the Knights Templar in Barcelona (1118–1312).

At the end of **Carrer del Timó (No. 3)**, a bricked-up door used to link the **House of the Templars** to the section of wall that led to the Roman gate at Regomir. This private passage that James I had conceded to the Templars is the only vestige of their convent, which was demolished in 1859. It ran for some 450 metres, of which 200 metres formed part of the ramparts against which the first houses were built. A central courtyard gave direct access to the chapel, its annexes and other buildings backing onto the Roman wall.

Built between 1246 and 1248 by Commander Pere Gil with the authorization of the Bishop and Chapter of Barcelona, who had allowed the Order to build a chapel and cemetery in the city, as borne out by a letter of 1246, the **Chapel of the Templars** has also survived and is now part of the Church of Our Lady of Victory, for which the Jesuits were responsible. Access is by **No. 4 Carrer d'Ataulf**, a short distance from **Carrer dels Templers** which crosses Carrer del Palau. All these names recall the site of what used to be the commandery.

This Templar chapel dedicated to the Virgin Mary has a single nave oriented south-west, in contrast to medieval building traditions under which it should face the Levant (east): it is in fact facing Tomar, in Portugal, where the Order had its headquarters. Inside, the nave is divided into six bays by five slightly pointed arches, equal in height and width at the clerestory. The apse is semi-hexagonal but the most noteworthy feature is the arched construction of the roof. Interestingly, this non-traditional plan is similar to that used by the Templars in their other commanderies (Paris, London and Tomar), in that it reproduces the octagonal plan of the rotunda of the original Temple of Solomon in Jerusalem.

The story goes that when Pope Clement V decreed the abolition of the Knights Templar in 1312, the bells of all their churches were broken with the exception of that of this chapel, perhaps because of the inscription on the door (*Domus Dei et Porta Coelis* – House of God and Gate of Heaven), which meant that it was a place of seclusion from the profane world and a passage to the divine world, where the Templar monks sought enlightenment from God.

Legend aside, near the old Roman tower known as Torre Galiffa, a small community grew up within medieval Barcelona, where all kinds of people including the Knights Templar lived in splendid surroundings. Later, after the abolition of the Order, their buildings passed into royal hands and became the Palau Reial Menor (Lesser Royal Palace), demolished in 1847 to make way for bourgeois mansions, attached to the palace where the royal chapel, originally part of the Templars' convent, was sited. In Catalonia, the Templars received donations of land in the Vallès from their early contacts with the Catalan counts. The first gift, dated 1131, was a property in Sant Pere de Vilamajor. In 1134, the Catalan nobles assembled to draw up and sign the rights and duties of the establishment of the Order of the Temple in the country.

A week later, a document was issued donating houses and land near Regomir castle to the Order. Over time, this site became the Barcelona convent. As these gifts were received in Barcelona, parallel donations were offered in the Vallès, beginning with a property at Santa Perpetua de la Moguda in 1150. It seems that at first the Templar headquarters in Barcelona was not a convent, even if it ended as such, largely due to the business that the Vallès commander carried out with officers of the crown. Several sources date this change to 1232.

In 1253, the Templars obtained permission to close off Carrer dels Banys Nous, which would soon become part of El Call, the Jewish quarter. In closing this street, they gained space next to the palace for a small garden, as well as exercising greater control over the Jews to prevent the esoteric knowledge of the Torah from overwhelming their spiritual jurisdiction.

Later donations of land within the city focused on Montjuïc. In the early 13th century, the area around the Roman walls saw people settling along the roads leading out of town in all directions and the activities of the Order therefore developed below the walls of its fortress. This encouraged the spiritual and socio-economic development of Barcelona, giving it an international reach while it continued to play a crucial role throughout the Mediterranean basin.

CAR BLESSING, CAPELLA DE SANT CRISTÒFOR DEL REGOMIR

36

Carrer Regomir
- Metro: Jaume I
- Fridays, 19.00–20.00
- Car blessing: 10 July

Blessed be your car ...

Each year on 10 July, all of the taxis in Barcelona queue up to have their vehicle blessed at this tiny chapel built in 1503. The chapel, dedicated to Saint Christopher, patron of travellers in general and taxi drivers in particular, was the first in the country to bless vehicles.

The drivers recall that during the 1970s, when the number of motorists in the city increased dramatically, as many as 2,000 vehicles could be seen waiting their turn for the blessing.

The tradition goes back to 1906, when Cristofol Sarrias, a pharmacist in Carrer de Regomir, and his friend Carles Bonet introduced the French custom of blessing vehicles on Saint Christopher's feast day. Only four cars were present at the first ceremony, one of them belonging to the artist Ramón Casas and another to the writer and painter Santiago Rusiñol.

Holding at most twenty people, Saint Christopher's chapel is so small (only two rows of chairs) that the font is outside the building in order not to hinder the flow of worshippers.

Nearby, at the junction of Carrer de Montcada and Carrer dels Carders, is the equally small 12th-century Marcus chapel, named after the philanthropist Bernat Marcus who built a hospital specializing in the treatment of travellers and pilgrims.

SAINT CHRISTOPHER, PROTECTOR OF TRAVELLERS

Reprobus was tall, blond and strong. As an adventurer he sought glory and made up his mind to serve a great king.

He defended the Romans and fought against the Persians until a hermit told him about Jesus, the most powerful of all kings.

Once in the service of Christ, he helped the weak and the ill to cross a dangerous river, until one day there arrived a particularly heavy child. The water was running fast and the child on his back grew heavier and heavier. When the man managed to reach the opposite bank, the Christ child revealed who He was.

From then on the man took the name Christophorus ("Christ-Bearer").

Saint Christopher died a martyr, beheaded. Needless to say, he was adopted as the patron saint of travellers.

One of his arms is preserved at Santiago de Compostela and part of his jaw at Astorga (Spain).

CORREOS, THE PHANTOM METRO STATION ㊲

Plaça d'Antonio López, s/n
• Metro: Jaume I

> *The lights from a phantom station can still be seen from the street*

When Barcelona began to expand in the late 19th century, Via Laietana, known as Via A, was built to lead from the city to the sea and it incorporated tunnels planned for the future metro.

The first phase of the Barcelona metro brought it to Jaume I station, the intention being to have the terminus at Francia station. Following technical and financial problems, it was finally decided to extend the metro to Correos, which was nearest the sea at the time. Correos station opened on 20 February 1932.

Then in 1966 the metro was extended to Barceloneta and, given the proximity of Jaume I station to the sea, Correos lost its usefulness and was closed for good on 20 March 1972.

The former corridor is still used as a ventilation shaft, as can be seen through the gate to the right of the entrance nearest to Via Laietana.

This abandoned station is also lit up at certain times, so it is easy to see from above, via the ventilation shaft that opens onto the street.

You can also see the phantom station inside the metro, from the carriage windows, between Jaume I and Barceloneta stations.

OTHER PHANTOM STATIONS IN BARCELONA:
Line 1: Bordeta
Line 3: Fernando y Travessera
Line 4: Banco
Line 5: Gaudí
In the Ferrocarrils de la Generalitat, Avenida de la Luz

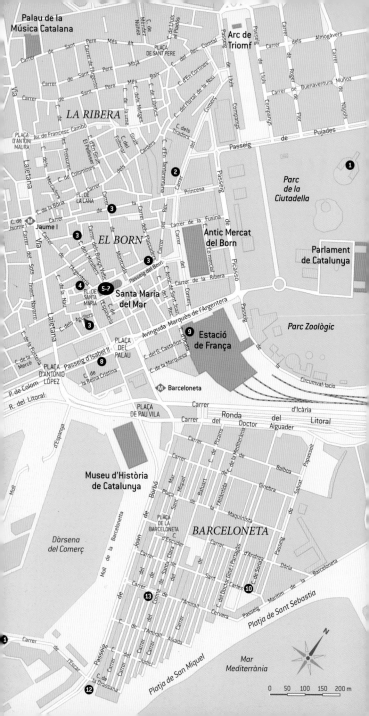

EL BORN - BARCELONETA

MASONIC SYMBOLS
IN PARC DE LA CIUTADELLA

❶

Passeig de Picasso, s/n
• Metro: Arc de Triomf

Gaudí
at Ciutadella

In 1875 work began on the great ornamental cascade in Ciutadella Park (Philip V's former fortress) for the 1888 Universal Exposition. It was designed by Josep Fontserè, a Freemason who won a public competition that attracted the leading architects of the time.

According to the plans, the cascade was to be 24 metres high and 70 metres around the base. It included seven waterfalls and a semicircular lake, oriented east–west, like all Masonic lodges. It drew inspiration from the Henri Espérandieu water tower in Marseille's Parc Longchamp (1869), of which Gaudí had kept some pictures. But unlike the Marseille cascade, Gaudí designed a cave behind the third fall from which to contemplate the water, as in the Artigas Gardens. Besides the cave, there are many elements typical of Gaudí – small temples, and salamander-shaped reliefs on the wall of the aquarium at the top of the cascade (true north) and the steps leading to the top.

As well as Gaudí, many others collaborated on the project with Fontserè: Cristòfor Cascante i Colom, another architecture student, and several sculptors with whom Gaudí also formed close friendships, including the young Llorenç Matamala. Gaudí helped his friend Rafael Atché with the installation of four dragons symbolizing the tetramorph (the four creatures that came to represent the Evangelists) protecting Venus (the Roman goddess of beauty, fertility and love) rising from her shell, the main statue of this monumental cascade.

Gaudí's first work was inaugurated in Ciutadella Park, on the terrace built for outdoor concerts by the municipal band, at the corner of Los Tilos and Los Álamos avenues. As Fontserè's designer, Gaudí was responsible for the stone balustrade that closes off the terrace. This site is known today as Plazoleta Aribau, in honour of economist and writer Buenaventura Aribau. Of course, the statue of the author of the poem *Oda a la patria* (Ode to the Fatherland) bears many Masonic references such as the cubic stone pedestal, the figure 5, the five-pointed star, acacia wood …

Gaudí would have been 24 when he presented the project for the iron railings for Ciutadella Park on 30 May 1876, signed off by Fontserè himself.

The railings are 1 km long and have 132 pillars and seven gates: one overlooking Carrer de la Princesa, three overlooking Passeig de Pujades and three Passeig de Picasso. The gate pillars are 9 metres high and the three auxiliary columns 4 metres.

The three main gates are lit by lamps formed by groups of six burners (now electric lights) protected by white glass globes. They bear the arms of Barcelona, crowned by the war helmet of James I of Aragon (James the Conqueror), without its characteristic winged dragon (James I was one of the protectors of the Knights Templar, predecessors of the Freemasons).

At the beginning of 1885, the gates were complemented by allegorical statues of Industry and Trade by Venanci Vallmitjana, and of Agriculture and Seafaring by Agapit Vallmitjana.

It is now known that many of the works in this park are by Gaudí, as this brilliant architect's signature was found during various 20th-century restorations.

MASONIC SYMBOLS
AT SANT AGUSTÍ MONASTERY

2

Carrer del Comerç, 36
• Metro: Arc de Triomf
• Tel: 93 310 3732

> *Napoleonic*
> *lodge symbols*

Freemasonry came to Spain when Napoleon's troops invaded in 1808, and various lodges were subsequently set up. The king imposed on Spain by France, Napoleon's brother Joseph Bonaparte, was the Grand Master of French Freemasonry.

Napoleon's supporters and the Masons of Spanish lodges proclaimed the First Republic in 1873, with the motto "Liberty, Equality, Fraternity" taken from Freemasonry and the French Republic.

They placed the Masonic symbols, including the square and compasses, on the three gates of Carrer del Comerç. In the early 1960s the symbols disappeared from the tympanum of what is now the entrance to the Chocolate Museum. On the central door, you can still see the initials F and M for freemasonry.

Tradition holds that the first Augustinian Christian community was established in Barcelona thanks to Saint Paulinus of Nola's visit to this city. He was ordained as a priest in 393, apparently under pressure from his followers. It is said that he founded a community, traces of which predate the Saracen invasion. This is thought to have been originally in Sant Pau del Camp and later to have found a permanent home in Barcelona.

In 1309 the Augustinians settled in Carrer del Comerç, on land donated by citizen Jaume Basset, a site now known as Sant Agustí Vell; they laid the foundation stone of the church in 1349. Construction of the monastic buildings was not complete until the 18th century.

The bombardment in 1714 during the War of the Spanish Succession damaged the monastery and in 1716 Philip V of Spain ordered its demolition to make way for his citadel. The Augustinians then settled near Carrer de l'Hospital.

The ruins of the building on Carrer del Comerç were restored by Pere Bertran (1738–48) and subsequently converted into bread ovens. The building was used as an army barracks and recruiting office from 1750 until the late 20th century. You can still see architectural elements from the former monastery, notably the restored west wing of the cloister (1473–78). Part of the building is now a civic centre, alongside the Chocolate Museum and municipal offices.

During the 19th century, a series of incidents threatened the community and its resources. In 1808 the building was taken over by Napoleon's troops and for a time soldiers and monks cohabited, but the monks left in 1813. The following year, the troops also abandoned the monastery, but the monks soon returned and started restoration work. However, they had to endure accusations of collaboration with the occupying forces. In 1835 the monastery was set on fire, as were the city's other religious buildings.

CARVED FACES IN EL BORN ❸

Junction of Calle de las Panses and Calle de las Moscas
Carrer de l'Arc de Sant Vicenç – Carrer dels Agullers – Carrer dels Mirallers
• Metro: Barceloneta

***Signs
of 15th-century
brothels***

In El Born district various faces of women or satyrs can be seen carved in the walls. These carassas (a Catalan word for gargoyles, although these are more like mascarons or grotesque masks) indicated to travellers or soldiers passing through town the whereabouts of the nearest brothel. The best-known carassa is a satyr below the third balcony of a building in Calle de las Panses, at the corner of Calle de las Moscas, a narrow alley that cuts through to the only nearby brothel. The three others are in the streets of l'Arc de Sant Vicenç, Agullers and Mirallers.

Being a port city, Barcelona was visited by hundreds of sailors and foreigners who set off in search of these pleasure houses as soon as they came ashore. The stone faces were the perfect marker, good for foreigners sniffing around as well as the illiterate.

In 1400, a number of brothels were already tolerated and protected by the government, and in 1452 King Alfonso V granted special permission to Simón Sala to open a chain of brothels in Barcelona.

The women worked every day of the year except for the Feast of Corpus Christi and Holy Week. At such times they shut themselves up in their workplaces and covered their bodies so as not to expose the faithful to temptation. They could also retire to a convent behind Santa Creu hospital, which was incidentally where they lived out their days when they grew too old to work – they had to be over 20 before starting.

The numbers of the buildings in which the city's first prostitutes worked were painted red, the colour of passion. Plant motifs were later added to the façades, making them rather too flamboyant, so Philip V decided that only the carved faces should remain as symbols of sated lust.

The brothels were only allowed to have very narrow stairways that would take up less space. These buildings were pejoratively known as casa de barrets, literally "house of hats", in Catalan.

NIGHT SHIFT AT LA PELU

Carrer d'Argentería, 70–72
• Metro: Jaime I
• Tel: 93 310 4807 • www.lapelu.com

Hairdresser
of the full moon

Since the days of grease and hairspray, La Pelu has been dressing and trimming Barcelona's most trendy heads. For the past twenty-seven years it has matched clients' hairdos with their body image, which is no easy task.

It has adapted to changing fashions and gambled on styles that have turned into trendsetters, copied by other hairdressers. La Pelu also offers extra services ranging from stimulating massages and talks to exhibitions of art, jewellery, and other objects, so that clients feel they have done more than spend a few hours at the salon.

The main highlight, however, is the night of the full moon. Once a month, La Pelu stays open all night, turns up the music, and treats clients to free drinks. They queue up in order to have their hair cut at this particular time.

Apparently, hair that is cut during a full moon will grow back healthier and stronger than ever …

FULL MOON LEGENDS

Many popular beliefs associate certain events with the night of the full moon: hair grows faster, criminals feel compelled to gratify their basic instincts (people with mental illnesses find their problems get worse), and suicidal tendencies are aggravated.

It is also claimed that a greater number of women give birth on the night of the full moon (although no scientific study has confirmed this theory), and certain gardening jobs, such as mowing the lawn, benefit from moonlight.

This is plausible because the moon gives off a considerable amount of luminous energy.

Some gardeners and farmers even sow their crops only when the moon is waxing or waning ...

Surfaces exposed to moonlight are also thought to become shinier.

BAS-RELIEFS OF THE *BASTAIXOS*   ⑤

Cathedral of Santa Maria del Mar
• Open daily, 9.00–13.30 and 16.30–20.00

> *The cathedral stone-bearers*

Built over an ancient theatre or Roman arena between 1329 and 1383, the cathedral of Santa Maria del Mar (Our Lady of the Sea) was the work of master builders Berenguer de Montagut (chief designer) and Ramón Despuig. It seems that the entire population of the fishing district of La Ribera took part in the construction of the basilica, especially the port dockers, the Ribera *bastaixos*. They carried the huge stones on their backs, one by one, from the royal quarries at Montjuïc, then from the beaches where the boats that had transported them to Barcelona docked, and as far as El Born.

The main door of the church is therefore a tribute to those *bastaixos* who helped to build what was originally the chapel of Santa Maria de las Arenas and which later developed into this majestic and imposing cathedral.

According to tradition, the construction of the church would take as many days as the number of stones carried to the site.

SYMBOLISM OF THE VIRGIN OF THE BOAT SCULPTURE ❻

Cathedral of Santa Maria del Mar
• Open daily, 9.00–13.30 and 16.30–20.00

The sea as a symbol of the world and of Creation

The cathedral of Santa Maria del Mar takes its name from the fact that the sailors and fishermen of Barcelona had from the earliest days commended themselves to the Virgin Mary and sought refuge in her at times of peril on the raging sea.

The name also recalls the Carmelite nuns' concept of *Stella Maris* ("starfish") that represents both Mary (by name) and the planet Venus, which has the distinction of being the planet most visible in the sky at dawn and dusk, so serving as a "starfish" to guide sailors.

The ancient Jewish writers clearly asserted that the sea is a creation of God (Genesis 1: 10), that He can subdue it (Jeremiah 31: 35), just as He can part the waters so that the faithful can walk through safely (Exodus 14: 15 *et seq.*) and arouse or calm its tempests (Jonah 1: 4; Matthew 8: 23–27). Thus the sea became the symbol of Creation and it was believed that the Creator was within it or that man was under its domination.

For Christian mystics, the sea symbolizes the world and the human heart as the seat of tumultuous passions against the serenity of the feeling of love. "I escaped the shipwreck of life," wrote Saint Gregory the Great in the year 575, referring to his monastic life (*Commentary on Job*). According to Aelred of Rievaulx (Ethelred, the 12th-century Cistercian abbot), the sea is placed between God and man and represents the present time. Some drown, others overcome it. To cross the sea, you need a boat, and union of the body is like a fragile vessel, while a couple's spiritual life is comparable to a sturdy boat. So that there are only strong vessels in both cases, people resorted to the barque of salvation, i.e. the Virgin Mary, because she was also wife and nun, mother of the Saviour and mother of humanity: most significantly we find her here as well, with a boat at her feet.

FC BARCELONA SHIELD

Basilica of Santa María del Mar
Plaça de Santa María del Mar, s/n
• Metro: Jaume I

***Barça
in church***

On the left of the high altar in the basilica of Santa María del Mar, in one of the windows that in theory date from the medieval Gothic period, a 50 cm by 40 cm Barcelona Football Club shield is displayed.

The shield is the work of artist Pere Canóvas Aparicio, who explains: "This dates from the time when windows damaged or destroyed by the Civil War were restored or replaced. Several windows were ordered from the company where I work as an artist. Some of them are new creations featuring my drawings, others have been restored. For this we were sponsored by a number of organizations. In the late 1960s, it was the turn of this window. Through the textile industry, we contacted Agustí Montal Jr, president of FC Barcelona at the time, who authorized the club to donate 100,000 pesetas, equivalent to about 12,000 euros today. To thank the club, its shield was incorporated in the window. The other windows also feature the insignia of their patrons."

WHY DOES BARÇA CELEBRATE ITS VICTORIES AROUND FONT DE CANALETES?

The Canaletes fountain (133 Rambla de Canaletes) gained its reputation several centuries ago, at a time when chlorine was not added to drinking water so it just tasted of pure water. The fountain's water ran from a spring through the channels (*canaletes*) of an aqueduct and was of excellent quality. It is said that when the locals wanted visitors to settle in Barcelona they would inevitably take them to taste this water, which made them fall in love with the city and bound them to it forever.

The upper stretch of La Rambla has always been one of the best places in Barcelona to quench your thirst. As large crowds tended to gather there, the end of the 19th century saw small shops opening up where drinks and sodas were sold. In 1908, Esteve Sala, an enterprising businessman and keen supporter of FC Barcelona, set up a new drinks stall next to the fountain that soon became a fixture for other supporters.

In the 1930s, the fans renewed their interest in this corner of the city — when the team was playing away, journalists from the sporting paper *La Rambla* (founded in 1930 by Josep Sunyol, another Barça supporter) wrote the result of the match on a blackboard hung in the window of the editorial offices overlooking Rambla de Canaletes, just above the Nuria bar. Crowds of fans were anxiously waiting in the street below, and if luck was on their side they took the opportunity to celebrate the victory in style.

The newspaper folded after the Civil War and the drinks stall disappeared in the early fifties, but the habit of celebrating sporting victories at Canaletes has endured.

FREEMASON SYMBOLS
AT 7 PORTES RESTAURANT

8

Passeig Isabel II, 14
- Metro: Barceloneta
- Tel: 93 319 3033
- Open daily, 13.00– 01.00 • Price per person approx. €40
- www.7portes.com • reserves@7portes.com

A restaurant modelled on King Solomon's Temple

Few of its many customers are aware of the secrets and anecdotes hidden behind the doors of this emblematic restaurant. The building is said to have been modelled on the Temple of King Solomon, and together with its ground-floor restaurant, it is full of Freemasonry symbols.

The signs of the zodiac engraved in the columns and the classic freemason triangle leave little room for doubt. Looking up, you can see the image of the Greek god Cronus (Saturn to the Romans), the lord of the Titans, and each entrance is headed by the restaurant's name written in different alphabets.

This restaurant, open since 1836, was for many years the meeting place for secret Masonic fraternities, hence all the symbolism. The interior is also worth a closer look, with a chequered floor, characteristic of Masonic lodges, and an acacia branch, a tree that Freemasons consider sacred.

Among other historic curiosities, it is notable that this was the first building in Barcelona to have running water. Also, the very first photograph to be taken in Spain was of its façade. In fact, the restaurant is on the ground floor of one of the city's most memorable buildings, Porxos d'en Xifré, constructed in the 1830s.

The man behind this building was Josep Xifré y Cases (1777–1856), a Spaniard who had made his fortune in Cuba by exporting sugar from the slave plantations to the United States.

Xifré later travelled to New York, where he multiplied his wealth. In 1831, he returned to Barcelona, investing his money in banking and real estate. The building and the arcades that surround the restaurant, which pay homage to his life, were designed by Josep Buixareu and Francesc Vila.

Above the main entrance is the following inscription: "Uranus observes the movement of the sky and the stars," and there are also medallions portraying the great explorers and conquistadors that Xifré tried to emulate: Columbus, Pizarro, Magellan, and Cortés. Between the arches, a number of sculpted trophies evoke his "success" in the Americas, including a cornucopia overflowing with gold coins, a chest filled with accounting books, and a slave's head.

FRIENDS OF THE RAILWAY ASSOCIATION ⑨

Estació de França (south entrance)
Carrer d'Ocata
• Metro: Barceloneta
• Tel: 93 310 5297
• Open Tuesday, Thursday and Friday, 18.00–21.00,
Saturday, 17.00–21.30
• www.aafcb.org

Miniature trains

F ounded in 1944, Barcelona's Friends of the Railway Association (Asociación de Amigos del Ferrocarril de Barcelona) is a dream come true for rail lovers. Located in the south wing of the França station, it occupies three vast rooms.

One holds the library and has specialized magazines, films, and over 4,000 volumes available to members. Collector's items are found in every available space: signals, telegraph machines, old posters, and hundreds of model trains, replicating both famous and little-known engines.

The second hall is open to members who want to run their model trains and feel like real train drivers. The tracks twist and intersect in such a way that the enthusiastic operators must be on their guard and employ some basic skills to avoid an accident in miniature. Finally, there is a conference hall where lectures and courses are held, and rail films and documentaries projected. The most striking aspect of this room is the seating, both for conference participants and the general public, which comes from authentic rolling stock.

The association, in collaboration with the Renfe/ADIF rail company and the Catalan Government Railways, organizes special outings to discover vintage and modern trains. The AAFCB also has its own collection of vintage trains, such as the Garrat 106 steam locomotive dating from 1926, the Berga 31 steam train from 1902 fitted with wooden carriages, and the Patxanga 304 electric train from 1926. During May, June, July, and August, trips on these trains are organized to nearby villages, where a stop is usually made for lunch, the idea being to recreate the ambience of an earlier age.

The association can be visited without pre-booking if you are just passing through. If you wish to join and participate in their conferences, excursions, or become a model train driver, the inscription fee is €30 and the annual fee €98.

There is a similar organization in Paris, with premises located beneath the Gare de l'Est (see *Secret Paris*, in the same collection as this guide).

THE HAND OF BARCELONETA ❿

Carrer de Sant Carles, 35 and Carrer de Soria, 18

A mysterious sculpture

To this day there is no known explanation of the origin of the mysterious hand sculpted in stone at the corner of Sant Carles and Soria streets. Located 3 metres above ground level, the palm of the hand faces downwards and incorporates two triangles that indicate opposite directions. Perhaps it was a bricklayer's joke or a stonemason's whim, no one knows for sure. But it has survived over the years and succesive restorations of the building.

The construction of Barceloneta started in 1753 and is the work of the military engineer Juan Martín Cermeño.

At first the houses had only one floor, until 1838, when a second floor could be added. In 1868 a third floor was authorized, and in 1872 a fourth. The house with the hand of Barceloneta dates from 1875.

NEARBY

THE CLOCK TOWER AND THE DECIMAL METRIC SYSTEM ⓫

At the end of the 18th century, the Torre del Rellotge served as one of the reference points for French astronomer Pierre-François Méchain's project to define a decimal metric system based on the Earth's circumference. A plaque from 1999 celebrates the bicentenary of his work.

Another point of reference for Méchain was the Fontana de Oro hotel, in Carrer dels Escudellers, where he stayed during his time in Barcelona.

BARCELONA'S FIRST MAN-MADE DISTRICT

Barceloneta was constructed to provide housing for fishermen and workers who found themselves homeless after the Bourbon conquest of Barcelona in 1714. Engineer Cermeño, putting his military skills to use, drew up a perfect grid composed of fifteen narrow streets intersected by five avenues. Cermeño, who later created La Rambla, launched the modernization of the area, always with a long-term vision, on ground reclaimed from the sea.

As an homage to the metre, architect Ildefons Cerdá, the man responsible for planning the Eixample district, laid out avenues Paral·lel and Meridiana in a fashion so that if their routes were extended eastwards and southwards, respectively, they would intersect at the clock tower.

For more details on the role of Barcelona in the definition of the metre, see pages 39 - 156 - 223.

A ROOM WHERE IT ALWAYS RAINS ⑫
SCULPTURE

Plaça del Mar, at the end of Passeig de Joan de Borbó
• Metro: Barceloneta

Five characters in a cage

As part of the Cultural Olympiad of 1992, Barcelona City Council commissioned eight urban sculptures from eight well-known artists to grace various areas of Barceloneta and Ribera. Some of these works, such as *Homenaje a la Barceloneta* (Tribute to Barceloneta), installed by the German artist Rebecca Horn on the sands of Barceloneta, have become authentic symbols of the city.

Others, however, have passed completely unnoticed by tourists as well as locals – such as the sculpture *Una habitación donde siempre llueve* (A Room Where it Always Rains), despite being the work of the Madrid artist Juan Muñoz (1953–2001), one of the best-known sculptors of the second half of the 20th century.

The work features five anonymous figures, immobilized from the waist down in metal spheres, oblivious to one another. They are shut inside a wooden structure reminiscent of the umbraculum of Ciutadella Park, set among the trees a few metres from the beach. These bronze beings seem to evoke the anguish of modern man, the isolation of those who suffer from loneliness while being so close to others, the melancholy of those who feel exposed to the elements in a world full of comforts.

In their apparent silence, the statues of Juan Muñoz challenge, ask questions and send a worrying message ... Is this why so many people pass by on the other side?

NEARBY

LESSEPS PLAQUE ⑬

In Plaça de Sant Miquel, to the right of the church, is a plaque commemorating Ferdinand de Lesseps (1805–94), the engineer behind the building of the Suez Canal, who lived in this house. In 1842, the insurgency that erupted in Barcelona was suppressed by the horrific bombardment of the city from the heights of Montjuïc, followed by occupation by the army. Lesseps, then the French Consul General in Barcelona, was shocked by these events and met with military leaders to halt the bombing. He also put the French medical services at the disposal of the wounded. A grateful Barcelona dedicated a square to him in the Gràcia neighbourhood, as well as this plaque.

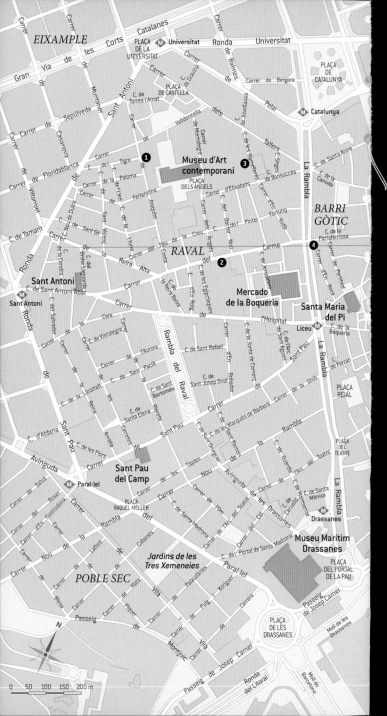

EL RAVAL

EN LA PRENSA DE AQUEL DÍA ...

❶

Joaquim Costa, 44
• Metro: Universitat
• Tel: 93 302 5996
• Open Monday to Friday, 10.00–18.00
• www.periodicosregalo.com
• Info@periodicosregalo.com

An original gift

I f you were born on 30 June 1974, did you know that a UFO flew over Barcelona that very day and made the front page of the Spanish newspaper La Vanguardia? And that on 22 October 1969, the first landing strip in Antarctica was inaugurated? Reading the papers of the last 100 years is addictive. En la prensa de aquel día ... ("In the press that day ...") has them all in stock, or almost all, as some dates are so popular that they run out.

This archival service was a natural consequence of the owner wondering how to make use of a vast quantity of old newspapers. She later acquired other titles and the small collection became an important historical archive.

Most of the people who come into the shop want to know what happened

on the day of their birth (or that of a loved one), or perhaps the day of their marriage.

So the staff rummage through the stacks of old magazines (vacuum-wrapped to protect them from humidity) until they find the relevant date.

You can choose between just the front page, the complete publication, or even an advertisement.

The shop also sells another original gift: personalized crosswords. All you have to do is supply a few details about the person you want to surprise: date of birth, tastes, habits, good and bad qualities, or whatever else you can think of to form the basis of an entertaining puzzle.

ANATOMY LECTURE HALL ❷

Real Academia de Medicina
Carrer del Carme, 47
• Metro: Liceu
• Tel: 93 317 1686
• Open Wednesday, 10.00–13.00

Barcelona's secret masterpiece of neoclassical architecture

Designed by the surgeon Pere Virgili and built in 1760 by Ventura Rodríguez, the P. Gimbernat anatomy lecture hall of Barcelona's Royal Academy of Medicine and Surgery is a a little-known masterpiece of neoclassical architecture.

This dark and gloomy place has an atmosphere that can be overwhelming, inviting silence and inspiring respect. The circular hall, while not very large, has a very high ceiling. In the centre stands a marble table equipped with a hole to drain away the blood of the bodies being dissected. Its proximity to the Santa Creu hospital of course made it easier to perform demonstrations on human corpses.

Notable among the operations carried out at the time (1770) was the spectacular separation of Siamese twin boys.

The benches where the students sat surrounded the dissection table. In the front rows were a dozen wooden armchairs reserved for the authorities.

A chandelier hangs from the ceiling and between the high windows are busts of a number of immortal figures from Barcelona's medical world, such as Ramón y Cajal, Servet, and Mata.

The building was initially home to the College of Surgery, then until 1904 served as the Faculty of Medicine. It subsequently become a training school and, since 1920, has belonged to the Royal Academy of Medicine. In 1951 it was listed as a historic and artistic monument of national interest.

Once a year, Catalan writers meet in the lecture hall to "dissect" the Catalan language, discuss the changing vocabulary, the future of the language, and additions to the dictionary.

Visiting is very restricted, with public access on Wednesday mornings only. It is no use trying to get in at other times.

There is a similar hall in London – see *Secret London: An Unusual Guide*, in this collection of guidebooks.

EL TORN DELS ORFES ❸

Carrer de les Ramelleres, 17
• Metro: Catalunya

*Drop off
your children ...*

At No. 17 Carrer de les Ramelleres, you will see what looks like a hole in the wall. Known as *El torn dels orfes* ("The orphans' hole"), this was where the much-despised single mothers of former times abandoned their babies to the care of the nuns.

The Casa de la Misericòrdia, founded in 1583 at Plaça de Vicenç Martorell, 300 years later became the *Casa Provincial de Maternidad y Expósitos* (Provincial Home for Expectant Mothers and Waifs). The hole, a sort of pivoting window into which the babies were placed, was in service from the mid-19th century to 1931. The building has since been renovated and converted into the administrative headquarters of the Ciutat Vella district. The hole, however, has been preserved as being of historical significance.

THE WHEEL OF THE INNOCENTS

As early as 787, a Milanese priest named Dateo is said to have placed a shell outside his church to collect abandoned babies.

From 1188, the first initiatives to save such infants were organized at Chanoines hospice in Marseille (France), before Pope Innocent III (1160–1216, pontiff from 1198 until his death) institutionalized the practice.

Witnessing the terrible spectacle of the bodies of abandoned children floating on the Tiber in Rome, he planned a way to save them.

Installed at the doors of convents and designed to preserve the anonymity of desperate parents, the "wheel of the innocents" consisted of a revolving crib accessible from the outside.

The baby was placed in the crib and a bell rung to warn the sisters who would then turn the wheel to bring it inside the convent.

Note that access to the wheel was protected by a calibrated grille that would only allow newborn babies to pass through ... This system was dropped in the 19th century but after a couple of decades had to be resurrected throughout Europe as the practice of abandoning children again became widespread.

PALAU DE LA VIRREINA ❹

La Rambla, 99
• Metro: Liceu

Viceroy and cradle-snatcher

The superb Baroque Palau de la Virreina (Vicereine's Palace) was built between 1772 and 1777 at the request of the Marquis de Castellbell, Manuel d'Amat i de Junyent (1704–1782). Particularly striking are the main entrance in the form of a triumphal arch, the balcony surmounted by a crest with the arms of Manuel d'Amat, and trophies evoking his military exploits.

The life of Manuel d'Amat could have come straight from the pages of a novel: a soldier at the age of 11, Governor of Chile (1755–1761) and Viceroy of Peru (1761–1777). While in Lima he was the lover of Micaela Villegas, *La Perricholi*, a beautiful Peruvian actress forty years his junior with whom he had a child. Back in Barcelona and immensely rich, in 1779 he married Maria Francesca Fivaller i Bru, a young lady from an aristocratic local family who was fifty years younger than him.

Maria Francesca, who lived in seclusion at the convent on Carrer de les Jonqueres, was really supposed to marry the viceroy's nephew, but the young man changed his mind at the last moment and failed to show up at the church. The story goes that Don Manuel, by way of apology for the insult, said to her: "Madam, if I wasn't so old, I'd ask for your hand." "Then why don't you? The walls and gates of the convent are much older and I put up with them," replied the girl.

Manuel d'Amat died in 1782, three years after his marriage, so he didn't get much pleasure out of his new palace, which was left to Maria Francesca – she soon became known as the vicereine although she had never set foot in the Americas.

ANARCHIST TAXI

⑤

- Tel: 620 20 91 20
- Not available on Fridays

The taxi that picks up nudists

An extraordinary taxi service, unique to Barcelona, which accepts stark naked passengers!

The driver, Mariano, naturally enough, applies his libertarian ideas to his service, which he calls the "anarchist taxi." He tries to promote "fraternity, solidarity, self-sufficiency, and direct action, as well as mutual support and fellow feeling."

Frankly, those who would venture into a taxi in the nude are relatively rare, despite the interesting sensation of freedom and independence that the experience no doubt offers…

Once they are inside, the passengers, dressed or otherwise, can choose from the many magazines or comic books on supply. They can also request their preferred type of music. Mariano likes heavy metal but does not force it on people. He has some pop, salsa, flamenco, and rock CDs available.

To optimize the exceptional service he provides, Mariano also has a selection of toys to keep children amused on the journey, and is willing to transport domestic pets…

If time allows, he can act as a tour guide: he knows the city like the back of his hand and is an expert on the subject of Gaudí's works.

Another of his services is called "Top Blanket." He keeps several blankets in the boot and often asks passengers if they have any to spare. In winter he distributes them to the homeless …

The fare is unbeatable, too. Mariano charges no pick-up fee: his philosophy forbids him from running the meter until a passenger is comfortably installed in his 2001 Mercedes.

Finally, and perfectly logically, Mariano does not always charge for the journey, especially when the clients are non-governmental organizations or involved in projects to combat social exclusion of the poor or other marginal groups.

LOVE IN A HELICOPTER

Bagdad, Tel: 93 442 0777; www.bagdad.com

Bagdad is Barcelona's most well-known cabaret, largely because it was the first place in the country to legally offer a pornographic show. The establishment also pioneered in organizing entertainment on board a helicopter or an aerostatic balloon. But for the more conventional clients or those afraid of heights, Bagdad has limousines for hire in the company of congenial young men or women…

EIXAMPLE

MAGIC SQUARE OF THE SAGRADA FAMÍLIA ❶

Carrer de Mallorca, 401
• Metro: Sagrada Família
• Tel: 93 207 3031
• Open from October to March, 9.00–18.00; April to September, 9.00–20.00
• Closed afternoons of 25 and 26 December and 1–6 January
• Admission: €12.50
• www.sagradafamilia.org

> *Subirachs' mysterious magic square*

On the Passion façade of the Sagrada Família, next to the *Kiss of Judas* and a series of sculptures representing various scenes from the life of Christ, is a magic square with a grid made up of a series of numbers, the sum of which is always 33 whether they are totalled horizontally, vertically or diagonally. Although in this type of grid the result tends to be 34 rather than 33, in this case the magic square is not the work of Gaudí but of Josep Maria Subirachs and fails to respect the usual rules – two numbers (10 and 14) are used twice and two others (12 and 16) are missing. Subirachs, who moved into the precinct when he began his ambitious project in January 1987 and stayed there until 2004, obviously wanted to emphasize the number 33.

The first explanation for this is linked to Christ, who according to the (sometimes contested) tradition died at the age of 33.

The second explanation relates to Masonic lodges because 33 corresponds to the number of grades (degrees of initiation) that a Freemason can acquire.

Dürer - Melancholia

Perhaps with the magic square Subirachs had wanted to hint at Gaudí's supposed Masonic affiliation, although this has never been confirmed (see pp. 189 and 193).

The third explanation for the square is as a tribute to Albrecht Dürer's engraving *Melancholia*, which dates from 1514. This work also features a magic square with the constant 34, which brilliantly places the numbers 15 and 14 next to one another, in that order, to indicate the date of its composition.

THE TEMPTATION OF MAN SCULPTURE ❷

Portico of the Nativity façade, Sagrada Família

A diabolical weapon

Catalan society of the late 19th century was deeply divided: much of the population lived in miserable conditions while the rest accumulated vast fortunes. Some anarcho-communist workers chose a "propaganda by deeds" strategy to denounce the dominant political, economic and social system through a terrorist campaign. Orsini bombs, a type of hand grenade designed to explode on impact, were used in various attacks.

On 24 September 1893, for example, Arsenio Martínez-Campos, Captain-General of Catalonia, was wounded by one of these bombs thrown by Paulino Pallás during a military parade at the intersection of Gran Via de les Corts Catalanes and Carrer de Muntaner. Pallás was tried and sentenced to death. When facing the firing squad, he claimed that his comrades would avenge him.

And so it was that on 7 November 1893, Santiago Salvador chose the symbolic site of the Liceu theatre to hurl two Orsini bombs from the gallery into the stalls during a performance of Rossini's *William Tell*. Mercifully the second bomb failed to detonate, falling into the lap of a woman who had already been killed. But the outcome was still terrible: twenty-two dead and thirty-five injured. Salvador took advantage of the confusion to escape, but was arrested in Zaragoza a few weeks later, in January 1894. He was taken back to Barcelona, tried, sentenced to death, and jailed in the Pati dels Corders at the Queen Amelia prison (in what is now Plaça de Josep Maria Folch i Torres, near Ronda de Sant Pau), singing the hymn to freedom, *Hijos del pueblo* (Sons of the People).

Following the Liceu outrage, part of Barcelona high society saw anarchists – and more generally the working class – as an example of the human soul at its blackest. Two years later Antoni Gaudí, a devout Christian, created a sculpture in a portico of the Nativity façade of the Sagrada Família, *La Tentación del hombre* (The Temptation of Man), showing an anarchist receiving an Orsini bomb from a demon's claws. As the proverb goes: "Weapons are the domain of the devil." Gaudí is emphasizing that Orsini bombs are part of that domain.

LABYRINTHS AND THEIR SYMBOLISM

In Greek mythology, one of the first labyrinths was built by Dædalus to enclose the Minotaur, a creature born of the love between Queen Pasiphæ, the wife of King Minos of Crete, and a bull. According to some archæologists, the origin of this myth may lie in the complex plans of the Palace of Minos in Knossos, Crete. Only three people were able to find their way out of the maze: the first was Theseus, who had gone to Crete to kill the beast. Ariadne, daughter of Minos, fell in love with Theseus and gave him a ball of thread so that he could find his way out. Dædalus was also able to escape along with his son Icarus after he was imprisoned in his own labyrinth by Minos. (Some versions say that Minos wanted to prevent Dædalus revealing the plans to this labyrinth, others that Minos wanted to punish him for giving Ariadne the idea of the thread.) It turned out that Dædalus' own design for the labyrinth was so cunning that the only way for him to escape was to fly out using the wings he had made for himself and Icarus from feathers and wax.

Although the Mesopotamian, Egyptian, Hopi, and Navaho civilizations all designed and built labyrinths, there are also examples located in Europe dating from prehistory. Other notable labyrinths built in the Christian era are to be found in the catacombs of Rome and in the churches of San Michele Maggiore in Pavia, San Savino in Plasencia, and in Lucca (Italy), as well as at Chartres and Reims (France).

These labyrinths tend to face westwards, the direction that evil spirits are said to come from (the west, where the sun sets, represents death). As these evil spirits are believed to advance in a straight line, the labyrinths are designed to trap them before they reach the churches' choir.

The relatively complex symbolism of labyrinths is also linked to the meaning of life, signifying man wandering through the universe, ignorant of where he is coming from or where he is going. At the same time, the centre of the labyrinth represents the safe haven of divine salvation and the heavenly Jerusalem – reached only after a necessary rite of passage that may be painful and tortuous at times. The attainment of this goal is symbolized by the flight of Dædalus and Icarus, which denotes both the elevation of the spirit towards knowledge and of the soul towards God. Ariadne's love for Theseus symbolizes love for another being, the two halves that permit an escape from the absurd human condition.

SAGRADA FAMÍLIA LABYRINTH

Mallorca, 401
• Metro Sagrada Familia
• Tel : 93 207 3031
• Open from October to March, 9.00–18.00; April to September, 9.00–20.00
• Closed afternoons of 25 and 26 December and 1–6 January
• Admission: €12.50
• www.sagradafamilia.org

An initiatory pathway

On the Passion façade (Carrer de Sardenya, facing west) is a labyrinth sculpted in stone, next to which is a serpent whose tail is said to symbolize personal fulfilment. The façade, also by Subirachs, has only recently been completed. In theory, it respects Gaudí's initial project, although it is difficult to be certain to what extent, because his original plans, models and sketches were destroyed during the Civil War. On the other hand, Subirachs' work has caused great controversy as it bears little relation to Gaudí's realist style.

"MODERNISME" (*ART NOUVEAU*) IN CATALONIA

The Art Nouveau style began to make its mark in Europe from 1880 onwards and as nationalist sentiment in Catalonia strengthened and drew closer to European rather than Spanish trends, Catalans quite naturally began to adopt "Modernisme", as it was referred to in Barcelona.

In architecture, Gaudí, Puig i Cadafalch, and Doménech i Montaner took the lead in making use of Art Nouveau's æsthetic freedom to create new forms based on nature and revamp traditional techniques. In painting, the best-known representatives of the movement were Ramón Casas, Santiago Rusiñol, and Isidre Nonell, who habitually met at the Els Quatre Gats café (Carrer de Montsió, 3), which was also frequented by Picasso, whose work of his Blue and Rose periods is considered to belong to this movement.

The name "Art Nouveau" was popularized by Samuel Bing (1838–1905), from Hamburg, who in 1895 opened an art gallery in Paris, called *L'Art Nouveau*, where he exhibited the works of most of the major practitioners of this new art form.

The term *Jugendstil*, used today to describe a particularly geometric tendency, was the original name given to Art Nouveau in Germany and Austria.

A German publisher, George Hirth, launched the satirical review Jugend in Munich in 1896. Its provocative style and original typography were immediately associated with the numerous artistic novelties of the period. Yet other terms were used to evoke Art Nouveau in Europe: Sezessionstil, in Austria, designated the Vienna Sezession (separatist) movement launched by Gustav Klimt in 1897. *Stile Liberty* owed its name to Liberty of London, a leading manufacturer of printed textiles, and this word was taken up mainly in Italy and the United Kingdom. Other, less-flattering names, such as *Style Nouille* (noodle style) were used by its detractors.

More than a simple artistic movement, Art Nouveau saw itself as a new mode of thinking, a new way of life, breaking with a model of society that it had rejected. It aspired to emancipate itself from the model of exploitation of working people, the role of the Church and of women, through the discovery of an eroticism and sensuality until then forbidden. Hence the many stylized representations of women's heads on the façades of buildings.

The golden age of Art Nouveau in Barcelona was between 1880 and 1930. In the rest of Europe, it suddenly disappeared after the disruption of the First World War, since it was incapable of producing buildings on a mass scale, yet limited budget. It could not therefore respond to the immense reconstruction needs of the postwar period. In Barcelona, however, the style remained vigorous and there began one of its most fertile periods in artistic terms.

BIBLIOTECA PÚBLICA ARÚS

❹

Passeig de Sant Joan, 26 principal
• Metro: Arc de Triomf (L1) and Plaça Tetuan (L2)
• Tel: 93 232 24 04 • www.bpa.es
• Open Monday, wednesday and Friday, 9.00–15.00
• Open 24 June to 24 September, 11.00–15.00
• Reader's card: €20, renewable every three years
• Free admission for students on presentation of ID

Everything you always wanted to know about ...

Everything about the Arús Library is distinctive – from the luminous and pleasant entrance to the coloured marble staircase and the word "Salve" engraved there to greet visitors. No specific style defines the place. The first impression, however, is a mysterious lack of proportion, with the rooms and their objects somehow seeming either too large or too small.

Before it was made a library, this was the private residence of Rossend Arús, a philanthropist, playwright, and masonic Grand Master, who believed that the only path to redemption was through knowledge. He died young (1847–1891) and his great legacy was this eccentric home with its extensive library on freemasonry, anarchy, and contemporary social movements.

All his life Arús thoroughly documented what was happening around him in notebooks that can be consulted in the library. The writings show his attempts to free freemasonry from any religious influence and to abandon the rituals that linked the masons with esotericism.

Founded in 1895, the library is crammed with curious details. At the top of the central staircase hangs a commemorative plaque in recognition of Arús' masonic work as Grand Master of the Regional Symbolic Grand Lodge.

Next to the plaque are Ionic columns and decorative borders painted with ancient Greek patterns, leading to a 2-metre replica of the Statue of Liberty, further underlining Arús' belief that the path to freedom is through enlightenment.

Arús himself is depicted in a portrait prominently displayed in the library, and by a bust near the exit.

The heir to a family fortune, he was bald, sported a moustache and was very elegant in his frockcoat.

He also wrote several plays. Visitors to the library can benefit from this inspiring place with its memories of Aeschylus, Poe and the other great authors he admired.

THE CYCLIST OF CASA MACAYA

⑤

Passeig de Sant Joan, 108
• Metro: Verdaguer

Barcelona on two wheels

Casa Macaya (Macaya house), now an exhibition centre for La Caixa bank, is the work of the great Catalan Modernist master, Josep Puig i Cadafalch (1867–1956). As a pupil of Lluís Doménech i Montaner, he is considered to be the last representative of Modernism and the first of Novecentismo (a movement seeking to renew standards while reaffirming classical values).

Casa Macaya, built in 1901, offers a superb homage to the bicycle, the most practical and rapid means of transport at the time.

On the capital of one of the columns, Eusebi Arnau sculpted a bicycle. There is a woman astride it, as Arnau wanted to leave evidence of how important cycling had been in giving women freedom of movement and therefore independence.

Although the bicycle is less important today, a network of cycle lanes has been in existence since 1989, the first of which was in Avigunda Diagonal.

The artist Ramón Casas was himself a great cyclist. Casas and his friend Pere Romeu were the owners of the renowned tavern Els Quatre Gats at 3 Carrer Montsió, where there hangs a reproduction of a famous Casas painting of him and Romeu astride a tandem. The original painting is in Barcelona's Museum of Modern Art.

NEARBY :

GARDEN OF PALAU ROBERT

⑥

Passeig de Gràcia, 107
• Metro: Diagonal • Tel: 93 238 4010

At the junction of the busy Diagonal and Passeig de Gràcia is Palau Robert, a centre providing tourists with all kinds of information on Spain. Few know that this late 19th-century mansion has a wonderful garden where you can rest, read, or simply just enjoy the agreeable surroundings. The palace was the private home of the aristocrat Robert i Suris, who commissioned French architect Henry Grandpierre to build him a neoclassical residence.

JOSEP GUARDIOLA'S INITIALS ❼
Pasaje de la Concepción, 4

> **Smell the coffee at La Pedrera**

Near Casa Milà (La Pedrera), carved over the door of No. 4 Pasaje de la Concepción, the initials JG are a discreet reminder that Josep Guardiola, a businessman who was wealthy enough to commission one of Gaudí's most famous buildings, once lived here.

Josep Guardiola i Grau (1831–1901) left L'Aleixar in Tarragona, where he was born, when he was only 17. By the time he returned to Europe forty years later he had amassed a fortune of 20 million pesetas, largely through Guatemalan coffee. He had indeed spent all that time in Guatemala, specifically at San Pablo Jocopilas where he bought a property, El Chocolá, in the mid-19th century. There he managed to produce one of the best coffees in Central America, supplying the most exclusive clientele. He was also astute enough to sell the property for a thousand times more than he paid for it, before the international price of coffee fell. On moving to Paris, he began to enjoy life in the company of Roser Segimon i Artells (1870–1964), a girl from Reus who became his wife in 1891.

Every time they went to Barcelona, Josep and Roser stayed at their house in Pasaje de la Concepción, which has since become a university residence.

In 1903 the widowed Roser, still in mourning, was staying at the spa town of Vichy. Pere Milà i Camps (1874–1940), a young man of the Barcelona

bourgeoisie with a reputation as a womanizer, noticed her. Two years later they were married. People were quick to point out that *Perico*, as Milà was known, had not married Guardiola's widow, but the widow's *guardiola* (piggy bank). Milà invested part of Guardiola's fortune in building a new house for the couple, Casa Milà, today one of Barcelona's best-known buildings.

NEARBY

GARDEN OF THE RAMON CASAS HOUSE ❽
The Modernist house of the Catalan Spanish artist Ramon Casas i Carbó, designed by the architect Antoni Rovira i Rabasa (1899), stands at No. 96 Passeig de Gràcia. Although the painter owned the building and lived in the main part of the house, another leading Catalan exponent of Modernism, Santiago Rusiñol i Prats, also lived here, as indicated on a plate near the door. To see what remains of Casas' home, go into the Vinçon shop and climb the stairs to admire the fireplace, garden and interior courtyard with its skylights.

DELICATESSEN QUEVIURES MÚRRIA ❾

Carrer de Roger de Llúria, 85
• Metro: Passeig de Gràcia
• Tel: 93 215 5789
• Open Monday to Friday, 9.00–14.00 and 17.00–21.00

Darwin's monkey

Filled with exquisite and often exclusive culinary treats, the shop window of the 100-year-old delicatessen, Queviures Múrria, displays a reproduction of a poster designed by Ramón Casas, a Modernist painter who was well known in Barcelona for his graphic designs. This poster was commissioned for the liquor *Anís del Mono* (The Monkey's Anise) and although it is not the original picture, which is in the private collection of the Osborne family, it is valuable none the less.

In 1898, Ramón Casas won a competition sponsored by the Bosch distilleries in Barcelona.

The winner would go down in history by immortalizing the Anís del Mono logo. Casas found his inspiration from the stir caused by Darwin with *On the Origin of Species*, published in 1859. He interpreted Darwin's theory – that man is descended from the ape – in a rather haphazard but effective manner, and wrote on the label: "It's the best. Science says so and I don't lie." Casas won the competition, and Anís del Mono became an unprecedented success, which other liquor brands have tried in vain to emulate.

> Queviures Múrria is a legendary store. It opened in 1898 as a coffee roaster and biscuit factory. In those days it was called La Purísima, taking its name from a nearby church.

NEARBY

THE CHURCH THAT CHANGED NEIGHBOURHOOD ❿

Iglesia de la Concepción
Aragó, 299 • Metro: Girona • Tel: 93 457 6552 • www.concepciobcn.com
• Open daily, 8.00–13.00 and 17.00–21.00

The church of the Conception has not always stood at No. 295 Carrer d'Aragó. It used to be in Carrer de Jonqueres, but was dismantled brick by brick in 1869 and transferred to its new home. The move and reconstruction, supervised by Jeroni Granelli i Mundet, began on 29 June and took two years to complete.

Originally built in the 14th century, this Gothic church had formed part of the monastery of Jonqueres, until the municipality reclaimed the plot of land for urban development. The parishioners succeeded in having the church moved onto unbuilt land with only trees and meadows at the time, but which later became part of the Eixample. In 1879, a bell tower was added from the San Miguel church, which had also been demolished.

GARDENS OF TORRE DE LAS AGUAS　⑪

Carrer de Roger de Llúria, 56
• Metro: Girona
• January, February, November and December, open 10.00–18.00
• March and October, 10.00–19.00
• April and September, 10.00–20.00
• May, June, July and August, 10.00–21.00

An oasis in the city

The gardens of Torre de las Aguas are a green oasis in the heart of the Eixample ("Extension") district.

A wrought-iron gate, designed by Robert Llimós and decorated with undulating waves, welcomes visitors into this relaxing place.

The idea of setting such havens of peace amidst residential blocks originated with Ildefons Cerdà, the engineer who masterminded the Eixample expansion. In fact, the gardens of Torre de las Aguas are one of the few places that survived intact from his original plans.

The magnificent and imposing tower formerly provided the neighbourhood with water, hence its name, and it is still a meeting point for local residents. Erected by architect Josep Oriol Mestres and engineer Antoní Darder in 1870, the tower presides over a small pool that is very popular with children in summer.

MASONIC EIXAMPLE?

Until 1859, Barcelona was surrounded by city walls, but at the beginning of the 19th century the city had begun to expand beyond these confines. The engineer responsible for urbanizing the zone between the old city centre of Barcelona and the Collserola hills behind was Ildefons Cerdà, a forward-thinking man also thought to be a Freemason, although there is no conclusive evidence to prove his affiliation to the lodges.

The grid of the Eixample, that extends the area between Avinguda Diagonal, Plaça de Espanya and Avinguda Carlos I, is composed of perfectly marked-out squares. Some believe that this obsession with squares in Cerdà's designs must be a Masonic influence. Whether this is true or not, his mission was to make the Eixample an egalitarian district, where differences would be obliterated and there would be no obvious centre of power, endowed with plentiful green spaces and recreational land for the residents to enjoy. The intention behind his urban plan was to stop the city from being a breeding-ground for disease, and ensure that the Eixample would be a light-filled area with patio gardens, trees, wide streets, and low-rise buildings, all rather similar in style, to give a sense of social equality. However, most of the ideas behind his project were not put into practice, as over time the real-estate developers disregarded many of its provisions on building heights and densities.

MUSEU DEL PERFUM ⓬

Passeig de Gràcia, 39
• Metro: Passeig de Gràcia
• Tel: 93 216 0121 • www.museudelperfum.com
• Open Monday to Friday, 10:30–14.00 and 16.30–20.00 and Saturday,
11.00–14.00

A museum in the back shop

There is nothing outside or inside the building at No. 39 Passeig de Gràcia to indicate that this place is any different to hundreds of other modern perfumeries.

However, ask any assistant about the Perfume Museum and they will point out a door at the rear of the shop.

The moment the assistant turns on the lights, there is usually a gasp of admiration upon seeing the display cabinets which some 5,000 perfume bottles, all arranged in chronological order, beginning with censers, perfume burners, and flasks from the ancient civilizations of Egypt, Etruria, Rome and Greece. These relics are the first stop on a comprehensive tour of the history of perfumes, which also includes miniatures, catalogues, and past advertisements and perfume labels.

The museum, open since 1961, holds an extraordinary collection of perfume containers, notable both for their originality and their origins, such as the bottle that once belonged to the French queen, Marie-Antoinette.

The story behind some of the perfumes is also revealed, such as "4711," one of the oldest brands, whose name derives from when Napoleon ordered his troops to number every house in Cologne (Germany), and 4711 Glockengasse was the house of a perfume-maker…

There are collectors' items such as the bottle Christian Dior had made in 1947 for the anniversary of Miss Dior. A limited edition of one hundred bottles was made in Baccarat crystal. There is also a bottle designed by Salvador Dalí for Le Roy Soleil perfume.

NEARBY

THE SPY SHOP ⓭

Carrer d'Aragó, 240
• Metro: Passeig de Gràcia
• www.latiendadelespia.es
• Open Monday to Friday, 10.00–14.00 and 17.00–20.30

Looking for sunglasses with rear-view mirrors or a device to listen through walls? Perhaps a bug detector or a cigarette pack with a hidden camera?

The Spy Shop, open for almost twenty years now, has every device you could possibly need for spying and avoiding being spied upon.

Some of its star products are a voice demodulator and a telephone the size of a fax machine that can imitate different types of speech: that of an old man, a child, or a woman.

Whether you are interested in joining the paparazzi or simply taking pictures without being noticed, this shop has a full range of options: screwdriver camera, pen camera, cigarette-lighter camera, calculator camera …

BARCELONA SEMINARY'S MUSEUM OF GEOLOGY

14

Diputació, 231
- Metro: Universitat
- Tel: 93 454 1600
- Open Monday to Thursday, 17.00–19.00
- Admission free

More than just a pile of stones

Located within the Barcelona Seminary, the Geological Museum is an astonishing place where all the guides, directors, and researchers are are Catholic priests.

Despite its tricky access through a maze of corridors and staircases, you should eventually find the museum entrance.

Founded in 1874, the museum specializes in palaeontology, with particular emphasis on invertebrate fossils.

It belongs to the Church of Barcelona and contains over 60,000 items dating from all geological eras.

All of the fossils are of great interest, and a guide who is both a priest and a scientist will explain how and why they preserve the remains of a prehistoric monster found in Sabadell, or why a jaw belonging to a hominid from the Miocene epoch is so valuable.

There is also a library with over 13,000 specialized volumes, and a laboratory for analysing and classifying fossils. Each year the museum publishes its own magazine, *Batallería*, where activities and new findings are described.

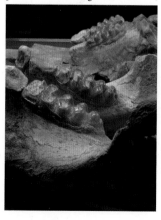

Most visitors are palæontology students and specialists. The priests complain that not many children visit the centre, probably because fossils do not have any gadgets or buttons to play with. In any case, it is advisable to ring before you would like to visit.

If you do get lost on the way to the museum, don't worry, you can always relax on the building's magnificent patios and balconies.

SCHOOL OF SAN MIGUEL DEL SAGRADO CORAZÓN

Carrer de Rosselló, 175
• Metro: Hospital Clínic
• Tel: 93 321 9664
• The cloister is closed to the public, but you can make an appointment to visit

Saint Michael of the Sacred Heart school is the unexpected home of a three-wing cloister (in the original plan there were four, but one was never built), which was transferred stone by stone from the Raval neighbourhood.

> *Stone by stone ...*

The cloister dates from the 15th century and not only has it suffered dismantling but also a fire during Barcelona's "Tragic Week" (Setmana Tràgica) of church burnings in 1909.

Now its gargoyles are at rest in far more peaceful surroundings, watching benevolently over the basketball games of the schoolchildren.

The reason for the move was the redevelopment of Barcelona's historic city centre two decades ago, in which some buildings and monuments were replaced by public spaces.

The convent of Santa María de Jerusalem, in Plaça de la Gardunya, was one of the victims of this renovation. Its original site is now the car park of the Boqueria market, and what remained of the cloister was moved to the school.

PULLING DOWN AND MOVING OUT ...
Other convents and religious buildings suffered a similar fate. In the 19th century, another great wave of reform within the city's old quarters affected many ecclesiastical properties. At the time, the Church owned close to 20% of the urban area including cemeteries, schools, churches and convents. What was not destroyed in the burning of convents that took place in 1835 and again during the "Tragic Week" of 1909 was expropriated by the city authorities through aggressive legal action. The transfer of the cloister of San Miguel del Sagrado Corazón is only one example of the metamorphosis that Barcelona has undergone in the past two centuries.
The most regrettable loss was the church and convent of Carme, sacrificed in order to widen Carrer dels Angels and give access to Notariat and Doctor Dou streets. The Liceu opera house was built on the former site of the convent of la Mare de Déu de la Bona Nova, while the Orient hotel in La Rambla is located on land that once belonged to the Franciscan college of Sant Bonaventura. The hotel has integrated part of the cloister into its dining area, where some blind arches can still be seen. The kitchen garden of the convent of San Agustí Vell has been turned into a square, and its library became part of the former Odeon theatre.

THE COMTE D'URGELL TRAFFIC LIGHTS **16**

Carrer del Comte d'Urgell
One at the junction with Carrer de Buenos Aires and another at the
junction with Carrer de Londres

*Designer
traffic lights*

These silver-painted traffic lights on Carrer del Comte d'Urgell have become a symbol of bygone Barcelona. They are the oldest in town, and although nobody is quite sure of the exact date, it is believed they have been set up here since the late 1940s or early 1950s.

The lights are anchored in a block of stone and, to add to their charm, are crowned by a streetlight.

Barcelona's first traffic lights date from the Universal Exposition of 1929, and stood at the junction of Carrer de Provença and Carrer de Balmes. These early examples had to be lit manually by traffic wardens. In later models the light would change when the passage of vehicles activated a rubber device.

During the Civil War, traffic lights were placed at Gran Vía, Plaça de Catalunya, Portal de l'Àngel, Passeig de Gràcia, Rambla de Catalunya, and Avinguda Diagonal.

NEARBY

EDITORIAL SOPENA **17**

• Carrer de Provença, 93 • Metro: Hospital Clínic

On the grounds where Ramón Sopena's publishing house used to stand in 1894, there is now a hidden garden. It is one of the few green spaces that has survived the city's urban reforms and was set up as a tribute to the publisher. Artist Jordi Gispert created a curious mosaic using ceramic tiles, sculptures, and other elements he rescued from the building's original façade.

A SODA SIPHON CLOCK **18**

Avingunda de Roma, 105

The concrete siphon at Avingunda de Roma is two or three times larger than life. It contains a clock and hangs outside a vehicle repair shop. The location used to be a factory producing soda siphons (Sifones A. Puértolas), and the present owner decided to keep the siphon clock as a souvenir.

Soda water was a popular drink during the first half of the 20th century.

It was often mixed with wine, and was thought to be an aid to digestion. Over the years, the availability of other fizzy drinks, together with the fact that soda siphons were impractical and slightly risky to transport, meant that they disappeared from the market.

AGRUPACIÓ ASTRONÒMICA DE BARCELONA (ASTER) ⓱

Carrer d'Aragó, 141–143, 2–E
• Metro: Urgell
• Tel: 93 411 2445 / 627 516 646
• Open Tuesday and Thursday, 18.30–21.00
• www.aster.org

For stargazers

Set up in 1948, Barcelona's Astronomical Association (ASTER) is a select club for those devoted to stars, black holes, comets, and anything else relating to astronomy.

During the 1960s, ASTER members were the first Europeans to tune into the signal emitted by Sputnik 1, employing fairly basic techniques. Since then, the association has acquired an extensive educational role.

One of their most popular activities is the beginners' course in astronomy, open to the public, which explains such things as how to use a telescope and orientation by the stars.

The course includes fieldwork visits to the Tibidabo hillside where you can locate and name the brightest stars.

Venus, Mars, and Jupiter can be seen, and on a clear night 3,000 of the billions of stars in our galaxy can be observed. These night-time excursions last from four to five hours.

There are also daytime excursions to observe the Sun (always carried out with eye-protection equipment).

Students also learn about astrophotography, and will get the chance to take home a magnificent photograph of the moon or a starry sky.

The course costs €110, and places are limited. (The price includes a guided visit to Barcelona's Maritime Museum.)

ASTER also possesses an extensive library and newspaper archive specializing in astronomy, astrophysics, meteorology, and aeronautics, and it is the ideal place to sell or exchange telescopes, accessories, or any second-hand astronomical material.

SCULPTURES AT CASA DE LA LACTANCIA 🄴

Gran Via de les Corts Catalanes, 475
• Metro: Rocafort

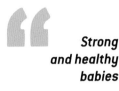

*Strong
and healthy
babies*

Casa de la Lactancia (Breastfeeding House) is all that remains of a service set up in 1903 by the municipal centre for aid to pregnant women and Gota de Leche (Drop of Milk) for poor children.

The renowned contemporary sculptor Eusebi Arnau was commissioned for the lovely statues in high relief that still embellish the building. Although the central element above the main door is the most spectacular (with the sculpture of a woman bottle-feeding a baby), there is also a really charming image of a toddler suckling from a kind of gourd on top of one of the columns framing the entrance.

Casa de la Lactancia was modelled on a French centre with a mission to eradicate the micro-organisms in breast milk that could upset the stomachs of newborns. The first home of the service was in Carrer de Valldonzella, where sterilized breast milk was offered to babies to ensure their healthy development.

In 1913, the service was moved to a small villa designed by architects Antoni de Falguera and Pere Falqués. The aim was to curb the high infant mortality of the time. The centre also offered medical assistance to pregnant women and specific infant care.

The building, now a retirement home, consists of a half-basement, a ground floor and a first floor. The pretty decoration is Modernist (Art Nouveau) with a profusion of floral motifs and stained glass. The central courtyard has been covered over with a veranda.

WEST

MONTJUÏC CEMETERY ❶

Mare de Deu del Port, 56–58
• Bus: 13 and 125
• Tel: 93 484 1999
• Open daily 8.00–18.00

Occult symbolism of the Batlló family tomb

The symbolism of the tomb of the Batlló family (the most famous of whose representatives was José Batlló Casanovas, a major Barcelonian textile manufacturer in the late 19th and early 20th centuries who was also behind the famous Casa Batlló built by his close friend Gaudí) is as interesting as it is little known.

The angel of death, on a pedestal surmounting the mausoleum, carries a scythe in the left hand and holds a chalice aloft in the right. He represents the guardian of souls, who is also their guide for this last trip from Earth to Heaven, from corporal death to spiritual immortality. The scythe stands for death and pain struck down, which is why it is lowered, while the chalice shows the feeling of love that persists over time, through generations of the dead.

On each side of the entrance to the tomb, an angel is set on a column. Seen from the front, the one on the left (male) carries the candle of spiritual

resurrection – the four candles that burn around the body of the deceased (the three on the altar represent the Trinity) symbolize the purity of the spiritual flame ascending to Heaven. The halo around the head of the male angel forms the Greek letter *omega*, signifying "the end". Seven stars are drawn around its inner rim: they represent the seven archangels in the Hebrew and Gnostic tradition (Michael, Gabriel, Samael, Raphael, Sariel, Haniel, Cassiel) who link man and God.

On the right a female angel holds a palm leaf, echoing the theme of resurrection of the soul. The Palm Sunday branches, like European boxwood, herald the resurrection of Christ after the tragedy of Golgotha. Incidentally, the palm of martyrdom has the same meaning, and the tradition of laying wreaths by the bodies of the deceased recalls this. The branches symbolize the certainty of the immortality of the soul and the spiritual resurrection of the dead.

At the feet of each angel is an owl, symbol of prudence (represented by the female angel) and wisdom (personified by the male angel).

On the lintel above the door of the tomb are two eagle's wings in the centre of which is a circular inscription of the chrism (Greek initials of the name of Christ, *Xpô*), which indicates the presence of the Spirit of Christ gathering unto him all those who pass the threshold of death.

SYMBOLISM OF THE TREES IN MONTJUÏC CEMETERY

Since it was opened, the cemetery has aspired to great aesthetic heights: many of the tombs face the sea and the choice of plants follows the principles of life and death, on the recommendations of Celestino Barallat, specialist in necrological themes and author of the unusual gardening treatise, *Principios de botánica funeraria* (Principles of Funerary Botany). According to Barallat, some plants are appropriate to a cemetery while others counteract the principle of eternal rest. Thorny plants are banned, for example, with two exceptions: hawthorn, which is synonymous with hope, and the wild rose. Nor are cacti acceptable, although some have been allowed as a metaphor for strength in suffering. On the other hand, cypresses, the magical trees of the Celts and symbols of woodland, are often found along with green swards of lawn, as in Paradise; abundant ivy; yellow everlasting flowers, which in Christian iconography stand for revelation and the herald of eternal glory; and finally the willow, symbol of sadness.

The Catalan etymology of the name Montjuïc is traditionally attributed to the Mountain of the Jews, and there is documentary and archaeological evidence that in the Middle Ages a Jewish cemetery belonging to the Order of the Knights Templar existed on these slopes. According to other sources, the name could also date back to the Roman era and derive from the Latin *Mons Iovis* (Mount of Jupiter), as mentioned by Pomponius Mela in his geographical treatise, *De chorographia*.

ADVENTURES OF THE METRIC SYSTEM

Not many Barcelona residents appreciate to what extent their city was involved in the development of the metre. Nor do many suspect that avenues such as Meridiana and Paral-lel pay tribute to this unit of length, and indirectly to the 18th-century geographers, scientists, topographers, and explorers who carried out the extremely complex observations and calculations required to define it over a period of six years. The task of making the measurements fell to two French topographers: Pierre-François Méchain and Jean-Baptiste Delambre.

Delambre was responsible for the northern part of the meridian arc, between Dunkirk and Rodez (France), while Méchain measured the section from Rodez to Barcelona.

Their "geodesic triangulation" technique consisted of tracing a line of triangles whose apexes corresponded to the mountain peaks along the meridian.

Méchain worked in close collaboration with two mathematicians appointed by the Spanish king: José Chaix and Juan de Peñalver. For six years, Méchain and his team travelled with their extremely fragile or extremely heavy measuring instruments, erecting what came to be known as "signal towers", often in severe weather. They were accused of spying and were almost caught up in a war.

In 1798, Méchain and Delambre met at Carcassonne before returning to Paris with their results, which, even though they were approved, failed to fully satisfy the Académie Française. So Méchain journeyed southwards again in 1802, extending the measurements as far as Ibiza in order to achieve greater accuracy in the definition of the metre. He died from malaria in 1804 and is buried at Castellón. Researchers carried on trying to perfect the unit of length until 1983 (see p. 223).

Pierre François Méchain   Jean-Baptiste Delambre

NEARBY

MONUMENT TO THE METRE AT MONTJUÏC CASTLE

②

• Bus : 50, 55
• Open Tuesday to Saturday, 11.00–14.00 and 15.00–18.00, and Sunday mornings. Closed Monday

In the dry moat around Montjuïc castle stands a sculpture honouring the metre. *La talla métrica de la natura* ("The metric measure of nature"), by Valérie Berjeron, is a concrete column 9 metres high, set between three trees with different rates of growth: oak, apricot and white poplar. It was sited here because the chateau tower served as a reference point for the measurements carried out by Pierre-François Méchain in the 18th century. The monument does not get many visitors – few stop to reflect on its beauty and the achievement that it commemorates.

MONUMENT TO FERRER I GUÀRDIA ❸

Avinguda de l'Estadi (access Palau Nacional)
• Metro: Espanya
• Bus : 50

> ## Free citizens of the future

In 1901, Francesc Ferrer i Guàrdia (1859–1909), a rationalist educator and freethinker, founded the Escuela Moderna (Modern School) at No. 56 Carrer de Bailén. Its aim was to produce free citizens of the future by offering a secular mixed education, regardless of social class. Ferrer i Guàrdia ended corporal punishment, insisted on the importance of children being in contact with nature and prompted them to question anything that seemed unreasonable. The Modern School soon opened branches throughout Catalonia, although objections to the project were growing meanwhile among supporters of traditional values, especially after the 1906 attempted assassination of Alfonso XIII and his bride Victoria Eugenia by Mateo Morral, a school employee.

In July 1909, during the *Setmana Tràgica*,* churches and monasteries were burned down. Ferrer i Guàrdia was accused of being behind this popular uprising, although he had nothing to do with it. Despite the lack of evidence, he was imprisoned, tried and sentenced to death. The voices raised in his support throughout Europe had no effect: he was executed by firing squad at Montjuïc fortress on 13 October 1909.

Protesting his innocence, he was taken to the place of execution with

his head held high and demanding not to be blindfolded … in vain. He died proclaiming, "Long live the Modern School!"

Ferrer i Guàrdia's reputation was justly, though belatedly, restored in 1990, when a replica of the Brussels monument (1911) that honoured him as a martyr to the freedom of thought was erected at Montjuïc. The bronze statue is of a naked man standing on tiptoe to proffer, with both hands, a blazing torch representing the light of rationalism. The monument is halfway between Palau Nacional and Palau Sant Jordi, near the escalator to Avinguda de l'Estadi.

In 2010, Avinguda del Marquès de Comillas was also named Avinguda de Ferrer i Guàrdia. Another gesture from Barcelona for a man who, as engraved on the pedestal, "died to defend social justice, brotherhood and tolerance".

*The series of confrontations from 26 July to 2 August 1909 between the army and the working class, incited by the decision to call up reserve troops to restore order in North Africa, is known as the *Setmana Tràgica* (Tragic Week). These uprisings took place throughout Spain but were particularly violent in Barcelona.

REFUGE 307

❹

Nou de la Rambla, 169
- Metro: Paral-lel
- Open Tuesday to Friday, 10.00–14.00 • Visits by appointment
- Tel: 93 256 2100
- Admission: €3

*A historic
air-raid shelter*

Visiting one of the few remaining air-raid shelters that protected the people of Barcelona during the Civil War can be a terrifying experience. Refuge 307 is a trip back in time, to a conflict that still endures in living memory. The residents of the Poble Sec neighbourhood took refuge there from the relentless aerial bombardment waged by Mussolini's air forces.

The site was discovered by chance during Holy Week 1995, following the demolition of a glassworks that revealed one of the three entrances to the shelter.

Built in 1937, it was one of the best equipped at the time, with electricity provided by a portable generator, an infirmary, sanitary facilities, and water fountains fed by the Montjuïc springs. In theory it could protect 2,000 people from the bombing, but as construction was never finished the actual number is not known.

Over a period of two years, 1,400 shelters were built in Barcelona, 288 of which were in what is now the Sants-Montjuïc district.

Today, little remains but a few scattered ruins. The renovation of the sewer system and the construction of underground car parks saw the end of most of these shelters. Refuge 307 is one of the rare examples to have survived urban development.

It was also the only shelter not to be closed down by Franco's troops. After the war it was used for growing mushrooms, as storage space for a glassworks, and as a shelter for the homeless. It was closed from the 1960s until its rediscovery in 1995.

Today you can visit the shelter accompanied by a guide who explains the main events of the Civil War and the efforts the citizens made to create havens where they would be safe from the terror of the bombs.

NEARBY

A STRANGE FAÇADE

❺

Carrer de Margarit, 30

A stroll through Poble Sec offers some rewarding surprises, such as the allegory of the industrial world on the façade of No. 30 Carrer de Margarit – a medallion depicting a woman leaning on a cog wheel.

OTHER AIR-RAID SHELTERS

Of the 1,400 air-raid shelters known to have existed during the Civil War, only a few have survived. Most were buried and rediscovered during development work or the extension of the metro.

One of these shelters, at Plaça del Diamant, is a network of tunnels with a sickbay and sanitary facilities. Discovered in 1992 during the renewal of an electricity plant, it is one of eighty-eight shelters in the Gràcia neighbourhood.

Work on a new car park at Plaça de la Revolución brought to light another air-raid shelter. It proved impossible to save it intact and only the sickbay and part of the corridor could be recovered. The narrow entrance is by a door within the car park.

In the Caollserola foothills, a millionaire businessman had built a residence named Palau de les Heures. The house stood empty after he died in 1898 until the Generalitat (the autonomous government of Catalonia under the Spanish Republic) took it over during the Civil War. Its shelter is perfectly preserved.

The bunker of the former Soviet consulate, in Carrer del Tibidabo, 17–19, is also complete. Inside its concrete walls are several offices, a kitchen, and sleeping quarters, all protected by two armoured doors that can be opened and closed only from the inside. Another private shelter was built in Gaudí's famous Casa Milà. Members of the Unified Socialist Party of Catalonia (PSUC, Partit Socialista Unificat de Catalunya) took refuge there. It was demolished in renovation work in 2000.

A manhole cover in Plaça de Tetuán serves as the entrance to another shelter that remains in an excellent state of conservation. Also worth a look is No. 6 Carrer de la Fusina, where the sturdy building, now a bar, was an attractive neighbourhood shelter.

Other shelters can be found at Can Peguera, at Carrer de Sardenya near the Sagrada Família, and the one at Avingunda de Pedralbes, used by the President of the Spanish Republic, Juan Negrín, when he resided in Barcelona.

Although these shelters are in excellent condition, not all of them are open to visitors, unless they have special permission.

Many of them are quite hazardous, and can only be entered with ropes and potholing equipment.

To visit the Plaça del Diamant shelter:
Ajuntament de Gràcia: 93 211 4973

To visit the Palau de les Heures shelter:
Fundación Bosch i Gimpera: 93 403 9100

TRIPE-SELLERS' ENSIGN

Sant Joan de la Salle, 42
- Tel: 93 554 4640
- Visits by appointment

*Sheep's
head
in Les Corts*

Embedded in the façade of some empty commercial premises is a sheep's head carved in stone, surrounded by a garland of leaves, which often halts passers-by in their tracks.

There used to be a butcher's shop here and the carving was no doubt made for the Molins family, known as "tripe-sellers", but who also ran an abattoir.

After the Civil War, they closed the abattoir to concentrate on selling tripe in Santa Caterina market.

The only reminder of that time is this strange sculpture, which has become a landmark for local residents.

NEARBY

HOME WORKSHOPS ON HUMAN EVOLUTION

Hominid Projectes Culturals
Parque Científic Barcelona
Carrer de Adolf Florensa, 8
- Metro: Zona Universitària
- Tel: 93 403 4476 / 630 621 930

If you have exhausted all after-dinner topics of conversation, you could always call on the services of Victoria Medina and Silvia Pintado.

They organize home workshops on anthropology, archaeology and biology. Their session on human evolution, which lasts an hour, is particularly recommended.

LIFE IN 3D: VIRTUAL REALITY CENTRE

Carrer de Llorens i Artigas, 4-6
- Metro: Zona Universitaria
- Tel: 93 401 2591
- Booking required

The virtual reality centre, a joint university and private enterprise project, offers the latest in advanced technology, in particular simulators intended for use by the military (war games) or in medicine (surgical operations). The centre is not normally open to the public, but does receive visits from organizations with specific needs and from keen students.

JARDÍN JAUME VIÇENS I VIVES

9

Avigunda Diagonal, 629
• Metro: Zona Universitària

Zoological sculpture garden

Jardín Jaume Viçens i Vives must be the most unusual and least-known park in Barcelona. Right inside the entrance, visitors are confronted by a terrifying metal sculpture of a reindeer being devoured by wolves.

Venturing further into the gardens, other figures of animals emerge, including a family of boars walking in single file, a rather disconcerted-looking deer, and a headless gazelle.

Hardly anyone visits this park to contemplate the beauty of the sculptures, which almost seem to have wandered in by chance. They are made from a variety of materials – marble, plaster, bronze – without any common style or scale.

Over time, some of the animals have lost various bits and pieces and thus been turned into mutants or hybrids, quite moving to see. This little park hidden in a built-up area is just next to La Caixa savings bank.

PEDRALBES MENHIR ⑩

Monastery of Pedralbes
Bajada Monestir, 9
• Metro: Palau Reial
• monestirpedralbes@bcn.cat
• Tel: 93 256 3434

**Guardians
beyond the grave**

In the Middle Ages, Pedralbes monastery was surrounded by immense walls, of which nothing remains but two watchtowers and two gateways, one to the east and the other to the west. Emerging from the pavement in the middle of the west gate, now missing, is the top of a curious stone known as the Menhir of the Angel. This is one of Barcelona's oldest relics. The legend goes that if you bang your head hard against the stone you should be able to hear the angels singing inside ...

In the Neolithic Period over 7,000 years ago, standing stones (menhirs) were sometimes placed in the role of guardian beside or under a burial chamber. The stone was there as protection from marauding animals, thieves,

and especially death – following the principle of the unchanging nature of stone, the soul of the deceased should remain intact indefinitely, without drifting away.

The phallic nature of prehistoric standing stones bears this out, the phallus being the male symbol of existence, strength and stamina: so when a stone was placed near the burial chamber it signified protection and oversight.

Menhirs were also used for capturing telluric energy which was then dispersed into the surroundings, usually for agricultural purposes such as sowing and harvesting (see p. 171).

OTHER BARCELONA MEGALITHS: AN ANCIENT DOLMEN IN SAGRADA FAMÍLIA?

There are historical references to other Barcelona megaliths apart from the Menhir of the Angel, although the stones themselves have disappeared over time. Near Rio Besòs there was said to be a dolmen (stone table) over which the parish church of Sant Martí de Provençals was built.

Close to what is now Montjuïc Botanical Gardens, another dolmen still stood there in the second half of the 19th century along the road leading up to the fortress, near the ruins of Saint Anthony's hermitage. A cross is said to have been carved in the centre of the stone, probably done by a monk of the time. The stone was destroyed towards the end of the 19th century.

At the present site of the statue of Saint Eulalia on Plaça del Prado stood a menhir of considerable size that the Romans kept as a way marker for Via Augusta. This road connected the imperial capital with the Romans' stronghold at Tarraco (Tarragona), and had to be cut through what are now Pere IV, Hospital, Mistral and Creucoberta streets.

Another menhir was located near La Rambla, in the inner courtyard of a building near the Canaletes fountain. This place, referred to as "Pati del Carall" because of the phallic shape of the stone, was well known until the early 20th century. Now nobody seems to know what has become of it, although the eminent Catalan folklorist Joan Amades, in his book *Histories i Llegendes de Barcelona*, traces it to No. 11 of the famous Carrer dels Tallers, under the name of "Pati de Sant Sever", which he describes as "a place of vice and drunkenness, a meeting point of students and soldiers". Amades also claims that in the middle of the courtyard, next to the tavern, stood a stone fountain – this just might be a relic of the much-sought megalith.

There is also a legend that Antoni Gaudí began to build the Expiatory Temple of the Holy Family on the site of one of 19th-century Barcelona's few remaining dolmens, which is now the crypt where the architect is buried.

As time passed and human society evolved, the names of many burial chambers were taken over by the surrounding area. This can be seen in the Barcelona neighbourhood "Camp de l'Arpa" (Field of the Burial Chamber), referred to in a 1037 document from the municipal register of Sant Cugat del Vallés in the form *ad ipsa archa*.

For an explanation of the role of menhirs, see page 171.

MENHIRS: ACUPUNCTURE FOR THE PLANET?

Telluric currents, caused primarily by changes in the terrestrial magnetic field, consist of electrical energy flowing through the Earth's crust from a depth of about 100 km.

These currents, the subject of scientific study since the 1930s (by Hartmann, Wissman, Peyre and others), rise to the surface along geological faults and underground streams and on emerging from the surface layers are counterbalanced by cosmic rays (mainly from solar radiation).

This equilibrium of terrestrial and cosmic energy is essential to human, animal and plant life on Earth.

However, when the equilibrium is disturbed, the population of the affected area may experience severe pathological effects (health problems). This is what can happen at a place that naturally gives off "good vibes" or "bad vibes".

This instability occurs either when telluric currents are particularly strong at a specific place (above the meeting of underground streams or geological faults, for example) and are no longer "cancelled out"; or on the contrary, in places where the solar radiation is not strong enough to offset the terrestrial radiation.

Some would have it that the peoples of antiquity intuitively felt these telluric currents and knew how to channel and use them by siting menhirs, dolmens and, more generally, temples or churches at strategic points.

Just as an acupuncturist inserts needles at precise points on a person's body, they transformed the telluric energy into subtly beneficial waves and rebalanced a site by diverting the surplus energy into the surroundings.

This is why many sites of churches, temples, springs and fountains have been judged conducive to healing.

Deliberately positioned in carefully selected places, they are loaded with telluric energy that can be absorbed by drinking water from the source or approaching the site in question.

There are many exceptional places around the world where people can "plug into" beneficial vibes, especially in Europe. In France, Mont-Saint-Michel is just such a place, as are the stone circles of Stonehenge in England and Stenness in Orkney (Scotland).

An ancient tradition holds that megaliths once sprouted from the fields like plants until the day when prayers cut short their growth.

NORTH

L'EMPORDÀ. ODA NOVA A BARCELONA ❶

Jardins de Salvador Espriu
• Metro: Diagonal

An "indecent, lesbian" sculpture

I n December 1961, to mark the centenary of the birth of Catalan poet Joan Maragall, the mayor José María de Porcioles unveiled the sculpture *Empordà, New Ode to Barcelona* in Jardins de Salvador Espriu. This work by the poet's son, sculptor Ernest Maragall (1903–91), shows two recumbent women, one naked and the other finely draped. Some people were quick to denounce the siting of this lesbian image in such a busy place, where passers-by might be shocked. Maragall had to accept this and see his work exiled to a lonely corner of the distant Cervantes Park. In 1985, when democracy and peace had been restored, his nephew the mayor Pasqual Maragall returned the work to its original site. It is worth taking a walk to Jardinets de Gràcia to contemplate these two women of Carrara marble from all angles, finding nothing remarkable about them other than their classical beauty.

OTHER "IRREVERENT" SCULPTURES

The *Font del Geni Català* (Fountain of Catalan Genius, 1856) in Plaça del Palau, the work of Francesc Daniel Molina, consists of four lion's heads (representing the Llobregat, Ter, Ebro and Segre rivers), four seated statues (the Catalan provinces) and, above, a naked angel holding a star. A few days after the fountain was installed, the angel's genitals were mutilated with a hammer and hidden with a stone drape at the request of the bishop, who considered it scandalous that ladies should be regularly passing by to admire the statue. Although the drape was removed in the 1980s, the statue remains castrated.

In Ciutadella Park, near the Parliament building, the 1936 monument dedicated to the Catalan volunteers who fought alongside the French in the First World War is by Josep Clarà. It features a naked man with arms raised, holding a laurel branch and a sword, symbols of the struggle for freedom. Naked, but not completely: during the years of the Franco regime, his crotch was hidden by a vine leaf.

CLÍNICA BARRAQUER ❷

Carrer de Muntaner, 314
• Tel: 93 209 5311
• www.co-barraquer.es
• Metro: Muntaner

**For your
eyes only**

The clinic of Ignacio Barraquer, a renowned ophthalmologist, but also an architect and inventor with a deep passion for design, is unique in the fascinating details it brings out.

Barraquer founded his masterpiece in 1941: an Art Deco building with a metallic structure and rounded forms.

In the foyer, an Egyptian *udjat* (Eye of Horus) protects against the "evil eye" and welcomes patients and visitors, who, if they raise their heads, can check the time from a clock unexpectedly fixed on the ceiling.

The waiting room is round and heavy with symbolism: walls are covered with the signs of the zodiac, Renaissance statues (some of which are decapitated human figures), comfortable leather sofas, custom-made doors and fittings, and mirrors positioned so that their reflections multiply endlessly, creating an optical illusion. (Some of these curious details can be seen on the website.)

Although the Barraquer clinic is visually astounding, paradoxically many of the patients are blind.

It focuses on the investigation, prevention, diagnosis, treatment, and control of all aspects of ocular health.

Although many patients will not be aware of the clinic's visual design details, they cannot fail to enjoy its practicality.

With the comfort of patients in mind, in designing his clinic Doctor Barraquer opted for curved walls, eliminating sharp angles.

He also chose soft lighting, which will not irritate the eyes of patients who have just undergone surgery or recovered their sight for the first time.

NEARBY

A GRENADE IN THE STREET ❸

An iron ball can be spotted on the outside of the wall surrounding No. 12 Carrer de la Granada del Penedès. You may wonder if this sphere, decorated with an iron star on top, is a grenade, a bomb, or simply a metallic ball. Most people believe it to be a grenade dating from the battles between anarchist and utopian socialists in the mid-19th century. This street used to be called just Granada (Grenade) street, but Penedès was added to avoid confusion with another street of the same name in Poblenou. Fixed to the wall with a metre-long iron structure, the grenade has become a neighbourhood symbol.

SCULPTURE OF ANTONI ROVIRA I TRIAS ❹

Plaça de Rovira
• Metro: Joanic

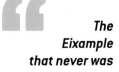

A bronze sculpture in Plaça de Rovira pays tribute to Antoni Rovira i Trias (1816–1889), the architect who in 1859 won the urban design competition for the extension of the city centre.

The Eixample that never was

Rovira was to have been responsible for developing the Eixample. However, a few months after his appointment, the central government in Madrid imposed the plans of Ildefons Cerdà by royal decree. Rovira was dropped from the project and had to be content with going down in posterity as the designer of the Corinthian column of Palau Moja, the Gràcia belltower, and San Antonio market.

NEARBY

MOSAICS, CASA RUBINAT ❺
Carrer de l'Or, 44 • Metro: Fontana

Directly opposite Plaça de la Virreina stands the Rubinat house, a building in the Art Nouveau style of the "Modernisme" movement dating from 1909, the work of the prolific architect Francesc Berenguer, designer of other architectural gems in Gràcia, such as the Moral centre in Ros de Olano street or the houses at Nos 61, 77, and 196 Carrer Gran de Gràcia.

The decoration of the façade and the ornamental balconies of the Rubinat house vary in intensity depending on the angle from which they are viewed, the tones changing from red to orange and from orange to yellow, giving the effect of a sunset.

CLIMBING UP THE CLOCK TOWER ❻
Gràcia clock tower • Plaça Rius i Taulet
• Tel: 93 291 6615 • Metro: Fontana

Not many people know the true history of Gràcia's clock tower and even fewer know that, with a simple phone call and a letter stating your interest, you can climb the steps leading to the belfry and the clock mechanism.

Designed by the architect Rovira i Trias, this 33-metre tower was built to raise the bell so that it could be heard as far away as possible, especially by those churches and parishes that had no bell tower of their own. The bell's peal became notorious in 1870 during a popular uprising against obligatory military service, known as the "Revolta de les Quintes" (revolt against conscription). They also inspired one of the most biting satirical weeklies of the time: El Campanar de Gràcia. The clock with four faces that now occupies the tower, so the time can be seen from anywhere in the district, was built by the Swiss craftsman Albert Billeter, who settled in Gràcia and made a reputation for himself with his innovative talent in the art of clockmaking.

FORTE PIANO

❼

Carrer de la Virtut, 13 A
• Tel: 93 237 0787
• Open Monday to Friday, 9am-2pm and 3.30pm-7pm
• Metro: Fontana

*Visit
a piano-tuner's
workshop*

Jaume Barmona i Vives is the best piano tuner in Barcelona. His discreet workshop in Gràcia district is home to collectors' pianos, antique pianos, grand pianos, upright pianos, and every other kind of piano you can think of, in the quest for the perfect sound.

Dismantling a piano and checking each component is like skilled surgery. Most of the time, problems are resolved by changing the filters or adjusting the mechanism. But considerable finesse is required when a piano is very old and pieces have to be replaced using a type of wood that is no longer readily available.

Forte Piano also offers advice on the styles and makes of piano, and what they are likely to cost. You can call in to ask questions or just to browse around.

NEARBY

A & K ORGUES DE VENT

❽

Carrer del Planeta, 12
• Tel: 93 237 6569

To build an organ, you need to be a carpenter, mathematician, physician, musician, artist, and artisan all rolled into one. In Barcelona, there are only two men who combine all these skills: Antón, who is a native of the Catalan capital, and Klaus, who is German. They are the owners of the only workshop of its kind in the city. They are capable of investing 50,000 hours of work on just one instrument.

The first organ was invented by the engineer Ktesibios of Alexandria in 250 BC. Since then, the technology has considerably evolved, but the time and patience required remain the same. Building an organ to order takes at least a year and costs between 70,000 and 90,000 euros. The main clients are churches, although there are some private customers. Antón and Klaus have recently built an organo di legno (wooden pipe organ). This is a very specialized instrument, made for connoisseurs and costing up to 100,000 euros. They also concentrate on restoring antique instruments. The last time they did this the job turned into a nightmare. The organ, dating from 1791, had to be dismantled in its original setting, transferred to the workshop, reassembled, restored, again dismantled, and finally moved back to be reassembled again in its final resting place.

The workshop is open to visitors, even though Klaus and Antón are not always on the premises.

VITRALLS J. M. BONET

9

Carrer d'Asturias, 6
• Tel: 93 218 2399
• www.vitrallsbonet.com
• Open Monday to Saturday, 9am-2pm and 4pm-8pm, or by appointment
• Metro: Fontana

*Makers
of the Sagrada
Família stained
glass*

For almost fifty years, customers have flocked to this studio workshop in the Gràcia district to order stained-glass windows in a variety of shapes and colours. Among the most extraordinary designs that the Bonet family has created since their enterprise was founded in 1923 is the multicoloured glass replica of a dog, commissioned by a Saudi sheikh to decorate his private mosque.

The family has also restored the windows of the cathedrals of Ciudadella of Minorca, Girona, and Seo d'Urgell, as well as the monasteries of Poblet, Santa Creus, and Vallbona de les Monges, while their non-ecclesiastical work includes Gaudí's Casa Batlló. They have also worked with great architects such as Subirachs and Grau Garriga.

Their best-known work, however, is without doubt to be found in the Sagrada Família. Since the 1930s, three generations of the Bonet family have worked on Gaudí's unfinished masterpiece. They made the skylight for the crypt, the windows for part of the Passion façade, and more recently, the transept. The process of constructing and assembling a stained-glass window is extremely complex. The Bonets first have to import the glass from Germany, Poland, or France.

Then, for the most specialized or valuable designs, they paint them by hand, transfer the design onto a template, and finally cut the glass to shape. The studio specializes in mounting and restoring leaded glass.

The play of light and shadow characteristic of stained glass depends on the thickness of the pieces, in which the Bonets are experts. Part of the charm of this place is that it is one of the rare craft workshops in Barcelona to have survived, along with several others in the Gràcia district.

NEARBY

THE MOSAICS OF LIVIA GARRETA

10

Carrer de Pere Serafi, 39 bajo
• Tel: 93 218 3405
• Metro: Fontana

The astounding workshop of Livia Garreta is concealed behind a blue door in an orange wall. Inside, yellow, green, blue, red, and violet tones dominate, and the shelves are loaded with the azulejos (traditional glazed ceramic tiles) that are Livia's raw materials. From them she creates colourful mosaics in the form of dragons, fish, flowers, or spirals, which are used to decorate paving, friezes, columns, and fountains throughout Barcelona.

THE FOUR FACES OF THE BOSQUE CINEMA **⑪**

Rambla del Prat, 16
• Metro: Fontana

Stony expressions

The stone faces on the walls of the Bosque cinema, depicting the artists Pablo Picasso and Isidre Nonell, the doctor Jacinto Reventós, and the sculptor Pau Gargallo, have a curious story to tell.

The site where the cinema now stands used to be part of the La Fontana estate, property of Joaquim de Prat i de Roca, which included private woodland.

During the second half of the 19th century, a great many theatrical and concert performances were given in this park until finally, in 1905, a theatre was built and named the Gran Teatre del Bosc.

Pau Gargallo was commissioned to carry out the four sculptures that embellish the front of the building. In 1998, after many renovations, it began to be used as a cinema.

The stone faces were also modified but they were retained as part of the conversion.

Passeig de Gràcia, which over the years has become a favourite place to stroll among Barcelona's bourgeoisie, was built in 1821. It was the first attempt to extend the city boundaries and link La Rambla with the Gràcia district, which was then at some distance from the centre. The route followed a rough track known as Camino de Jesús (Jesus' Road). Work was interrupted in 1823 and started again in 1827, to employ men who had lost their jobs during the depression of the 1820s.

A MASTERPIECE OF DESIGN

Vía Augusta, 128
• Metro: Lesseps

> *Barcelona's Clockwork Orange*

The lobby of No. 128 Vía Augusta is well worth a visit. This office and residential block, designed by Antoni de Moragas in the 1970s, combines wood, concrete and vividly coloured ceramic tiles. Its extravagant entrance could well have been the setting for Kubrick's Clockwork Orange or one of the retro lounge bars that are currently back in vogue.

Antoni de Moragas (1913–1985), an extremely innovative architect and industrial designer, headed Catalonia's post-war architectural movement and was dean of the Colegio Oficial de Arquitectos de Catalunya y Baleares, the profession's governing body. His work focused on Barcelona's urban development programme and he designed many residential blocks, private homes, and the community centre on Carrer de Gomis. He also supervised the renovation of the Fémina cinema.

NEARBY

VILLA MAYFAIR: A TASTE OF LONDON IN THE HEART OF BARCELONA ⓭
Vía Augusta, 240

On one of the city's main thoroughfares, Villa Mayfair is built in the most traditional English style, standing out among other more conventional homes. Its construction fulfilled its English owner's desire to import some of his country's architectural values.

VILLA URANIA: HOUSE OF THE ASTEROIDS ⓮
Carrer de Saragossa, 29
• Metro: Lesseps

Now a nursery school, seventy years ago Casa de los Asteroides was the home of Barcelona's most distinguished astronomer, Josep Comas y Solá. A close look reveals an isolated tower in the middle of the garden. This is the observation tower built in the 1920s, allowing the astronomer to study comets, solar eclipses, the planets Jupiter and Saturn, and to discover a total of eleven asteroids (one of which he called Barcelona).

The building, next door to a squat, is simple in construction but very typical of its time, with neoclassical ornamental details.

"ALABA POR" INSCRIPTION

15

Carrer d'Olot, 3
• Metro: Lesseps

*Gaudí's
occult symbolism*

At the entrance to Carrer d'Olot in Park Güell (built between 1900 and 1914), to the left of one of the crenellations round the perimeter walls, are the words ALABA POR.

This inscription seems to be an anagram of the phrase LABOR PAA. An 1871 Masonic manual explains that PAA (Principal Asamblea Auspiciada) means "guest house" or "lodge". A lodge is, of course, the workshop or temple where Masons meet to carry out their work.

So the plaque refers to the Labour Lodge.

One of Gaudí's biographers, Carandell, further claimed to have discovered the foundation deeds of the Labour Lodge, which mentions two well-known names: Antoni Gaudí and Eusebi Güell.

The letter K, which is found in the word "park" and appears in the fourteen medallions around the walls, suggests that Park Güell is styled after parks in England, the home of Freemasonry. The park name is itself surrounded by a five-pointed star (pentagram), an esoteric symbol often used by Masons (see the following double-page spread).

For an esoteric portrait of Gaudí, see p. 193.

THE STAR HEXAGRAM: A MAGICAL TALISMAN?

The hexagram – also known as the Star of David or the Shield of David – comprises two interlaced equilateral triangles, one pointing upwards and the other downwards. It symbolises the combination of man's spiritual and human nature. The six points correspond to the six directions in space (north, south, east and west, together with zenith and nadir) and also refer to the complete universal cycle of the six days of creation (the seventh day being when the Creator rested). Hence, the hexagram became the symbol of the macrocosm (its six angles of 60° totalling 360°) and of the union between mankind and its creator. If, as laid down in the Old Testament (*Deuteronomy* 6:4–9), the hexagram (*mezuzah* in Hebrew) is often placed at the entrance to a Jewish home, it was also adopted as an amulet by Christians and Muslims. So it is far from being an exclusively Jewish symbol. In both the Koran (38:32 et seq.) and *The Thousand and One Nights*, it is described as an indestructible talisman that affords God's blessing and offers total protection against the spirits of the natural world, the djinns. The hexagram also often appears in the windows and pediments of Christian churches, as a symbolic reference to the universal soul. In this case, that soul is represented by Christ – or, sometimes, by the pair of Christ (upright triangle) and the Virgin (inverted triangle); the result of the interlacing of the two is God the Father Almighty. The hexagram is also found in the mediated form of a lamp with six branches or a six-section rose window.

Although present in the synagogue of Capernaum (third century AD), the hexagram does not really make its appearance in rabbinical literature until 1148 – in the *Eshkol Hakofer* written by the Karaite* scholar Judah Ben Elijah. In Chapter 242 its mystical and apotropaic (evil-averting) qualities are described, with the actual words then often being engraved on amulets: "And the names of the seven angels were written on the *mazuzah* … The Everlasting will protect you and this symbol called the Shield of David contains, at the end of the *mezuzah*, the written name of all the angels."

In the thirteenth century, the hexagram also became an attribute of one of the seven magic names of Metatron, the angel of the divine presence associated with the archangel Michael (head of the heavenly host and the closest to God the Father).

The identification of Judaism with the Star of David began in the Middle Ages. In 1354 King Karel IV of Bohemia granted the Jewish community of Prague the privilege of putting the symbol on their banner. The Jews embroidered a gold star on a red background to form a standard that became known as the Flag of King David (*Maghen David*) and was adopted as the official symbol of Jewish synagogues. By the nineteenth century, the symbol had spread throughout the Jewish community. Jewish mysticism has it that the origin of the hexagram was directly linked with the flowers that adorn the *menorah***: irises with six petals. For those who believe this origin, the hexagram came directly from the hands of the God of Israel, the six-petal iris not only reassembling the Star of David in general form but also being associated with the people of Israel in the *Song of Songs*.

As well as offering protection, the hexagram was believed to have magical powers. This reputation originates in the famous *Clavicula Salomonis* (Key of Solomon), a grimoire (textbook of magic) attributed to Solomon himself but, in all likelihood, produced during the Middle Ages. The anonymous texts probably came from one of the numerous Jewish schools of the Kabbalah that then existed in Europe, for the work is clearly inspired by the teachings of the Talmud and the Jewish faith. The *Clavicula* contains a collection of thirty-six pentacles (themselves symbols rich in magic and esoteric significance) which were intended to enable communication between the physical world and the different levels of the soul. There are various versions of the text, in numerous translations, and the content varies between them. However, most of the surviving texts date from the sixteenth and seventeenth centuries – although there is a Greek translation dating from the fifteenth.

In Tibet and India, the Buddhists and Hindus read this universal symbol of the hexagram in terms of the creator and his creation, while the Brahmins hold it to be the symbol of the god Vishnu. Originally, the two triangles were in green (upright triangle) and red (inverted triangle). Subsequently, these colours became black and white, the former representing the spirit, the latter the material world. For the Hindus, the upright triangle is associated with Shiva, Vishnu and Brahma (corresponding to the Christian God the Father, Son and Holy Ghost). The Son (Vishnu) can be seen to always occupy the middle position, being the intercessor between things divine and things earthly.

*qara'im or bnei mikra: "he who follows the Scriptures". Karaism is a branch of Judaism that defends the sole authority of the Hebrew Scripture as the source of divine revelation, thus repudiating oral tradition.
**Menorah – the multibranched candelabra used in the rituals of Judaism. The arms of the seven-branched menorah, one of the oldest symbols of the Jewish faith, represent the seven archangels before the Throne of God: Michael, Gabriel, Samuel, Raphael, Zadkiel, Anael and Kassiel.

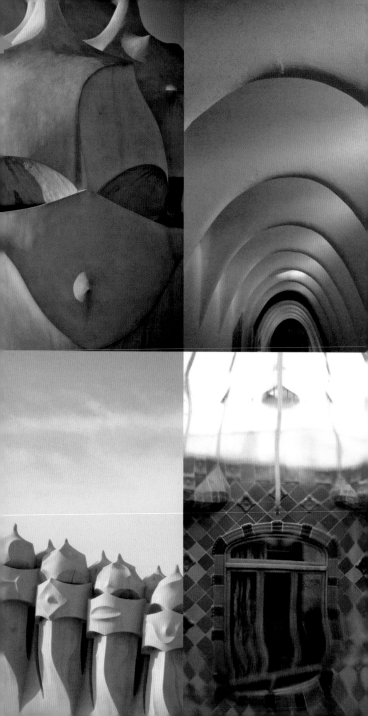

ESOTERIC GAUDÍ

There are many rumours about Antoni Gaudí i Cornet: that he was a member of the Masonic order of the Rose Croix, that he took drugs, that he was a blasphemer, that he was a saint, that he died a virgin, and so on. The theory most often heard and given most credence concerns his links with the world of Freemasonry.

According to Ernesto Milá, author of Guía de la Barcelona Mágica (Guide to Magic Barcelona), dozens of Masonic symbols can be found in Gaudí's work: the wrought-iron dragon in Park Güell is made from antimony, the alchemists' metal; the pelican of the Sagrada Família might be there as a tribute to the 18th degree of the Masonic order (final degree of the Rose Croix).

Some quirks of Gaudí's personality did in fact give rise to plenty of gossip. In his early career, he was thought to be arrogant, haughty, and self-opinionated. As the years went by, however, he became ascetic, very religious (he was a great admirer of Saint Anthony of Egypt, the founder of Christian monasticism), and a follower of the principles of Abbot Kneipp, a German priest, the discoverer of hydrotherapy and a practitioner of what is now referred to as alternative medicine.

Gaudí was very fond of meditating and gave himself up to fasting with such dedication that his usual diet became a few lettuce leaves and endives with olive oil. He gradually detached himself from material things, although the main body of his work was commissioned or sponsored by rich families. He always dressed in an extremely austere fashion.

Gaudí did frequent a number of Masonic circles and his biographers have detected markedly esoteric symbols in his work. For example, the plans of the workers' cooperative at Mataró, for which he drew up plans on a scale of 1:666, recall the number inevitably linked to the Antichrist and the Beast of the Apocalypse. Confronted with these arguments, his defenders have always fallen back on the close relationship he maintained with the Church, denying any links with Masonic lodges.

When Gaudí died it was almost in obscurity: he was run over by a tram at the corner of the Gran Vía and Carrer de Bailén and taken to a public hospital. As he had no means of identification, the medical staff took some time to realize that this gravely injured old man was actually the most famous architect in Barcelona.

To learn more about Gaudí's connection to freemasonry, see p. 189.

CASA MULEY AFID 🔟⑯

Passeig de la Bonanova, 55
Av. Tibidabo FGC (Ferrocarriles de la Generalitat de Catalunya)
• Open only for administrative procedures

The sultan's palace

Fleeing political struggles that were to cost him the throne of Morocco, Sultan Abdelhafid arrived in Barcelona in 1912. The presence of such an exotic character – womanizer, cabaret lover and all-night partygoer – intrigued Barcelona.

Perhaps to make up for his eccentricities, the sultan used to throw coins down onto curious passers-by from the balcony of the Oriente hotel where he was staying. Likewise, to win over the children, in 1914 he presented the zoo with a new elephant to replace the elderly Avi who had just died. A few months later, the city paid tribute to him and grateful children went down to La Rambla to applaud. The elephant, named Júlia, became the zoo's greatest attraction until the horrors of war intervened.

In 1915, the sultan left the hotel and moved into the mansion recently built for him in Passeig de la Bonanova by Josep Puig i Cadafalch. Although Moulay Abdelhafid left Barcelona two years later, the mansion is still there: it was restored after years of neglect and now houses the Mexican consulate.

The building is oriental in style, with ornate façades of brick and sgraffito, surrounded by a garden and flanked by a tower. The interior has retained its Modernist decor and an antique clock that still shows the time at which it stopped: 2 o'clock in the afternoon, one day in January 1939. At that very moment the concierge of the consulate, then on Rambla de Catalunya, had taken the clock down for safekeeping as the diplomats rushed to abandon a city about to be taken by Franco. The clock survived, becoming a symbol of the friendship between Mexico and Spanish democracy, while the mansion remains in memory of a sultan who lived out a bitter-sweet exile in a northern town called Barcelona.

NEARBY

TRAMVIA BLAU ⑰

The Tramvia Blau (Blue Tramway) connects Av. Tibidabo FGC station (Plaça Kennedy) with the Tibidabo funicular (Plaça del Doctor Andreu) at weekends, public holidays and during the summer. This line, opened in 1901, is the only one that still runs century-old streetcars that are genuine museum pieces.

MUSEUM OF ANTIQUE AUTOMATS TIBIDABO AMUSEMENT PARK

Plaça del Tibidabo, 3–4
• Tel: 93 211 7942
• Open weekends • Admission fee: free to €24
• Bus to Tibidabo departs from Plaça Catalunya

Historic attractions

At the touch of a button, you can activate a miniature ski station, a guitarist, a mandolin-playing clown, or a roller coaster. These are just a few of the most extraordinary devices at Tibidabo's Automat Museum.

They are all collectors' items in perfect condition and date from the late 19th century. Most of them, such as the tightrope walkers, the guillotine (which demonstrates the precise moment of decapitation), and the mechanics' workshop, are veritable relics of a bygone age.

To visit the museum you need to pay the park's general admission fee, but this is no ordinary amusement park, as most attractions date from the 1970s and have a very different feeling and style to their modern counterparts. Located at the top of Tibidabo mountain, at an altitude of 512 metres (the highest point of the Collserola range), its strange name stems from the Latin *tibi dabo* ("I will give you"), the words spoken by the Devil in his splendid vanity when he tried to tempt Jesus as they looked down on all the kingdoms of the world. Tibidabo does in fact offer the most spectacular views – particularly on a clear day when the wind has blown away the grey-brown cloud of pollution floating over the city.

> When visiting the Tibidabo amusement park, it is also worth checking out the Marionetarium, which gives inventive performances using vintage puppets.

NEARBY

FOSTER'S SCENIC VIEWPOINT

Carretera de Vallvidrera al Tibidabo
• Tel: 93 211 7942
• Guided tours with technical commentary can be booked

Most people will be familiar with Norman Foster's Torre de Collserola, famous from Barcelona's 1992 Olympic Games, but few know that it is possible to gain access to its highest point and enjoy fantastic views of the city, weather permitting. The 288-metre tower is at the top of a natural peak already 445 metres above sea level, which add up to a truly spectacular vantage point.

A panoramic elevator travels 135 metres in 2½ minutes to reach the top.

EAST

PAVELLÓ DE LA REPÚBLICA ❶

Avinguda Cardenal Vidal i Barraquer, 34–36
• www.bib.ub.edu/biblioteques/pavello-republica
• Metro: Montbau

I t is not generally known that Picasso's celebrated *Guernica* was painted for the Paris International Exposition of 1937.

During the Civil War, the Spanish Republic participated in the Expo with a pavilion designed by rationalist architects Josep Lluís Sert and Luis Lacasa, whose Modernist vision pulled in the visitors.

Replica of the space for which Picasso painted Guernica

The Pavilion of the Republic, at the Trocadero gardens in Paris, displayed *Guernica* along with other works such as Joan Miró's *El Segador* (The Reaper) and *Fuente de Mercurio* (Mercury Fountain), a mobile by Alexander Calder in tribute to the Almadén miners that can be seen today at Barcelona's Miró Foundation. The sculptures included *La Montserrat* by Julio González and *El pueblo español tiene un camino que conduce a una estrella* (The Spanish People Have a Path that Leads to a Star) by Alberto Sánchez, symbols of the struggle for freedom. These works by leading artists became testimonials to the tragic situation of the Spanish people, as well as a cry for help addressed to international public opinion.

A replica of this pavilion, the Pavelló de la República, was built for the 1992 Olympic Games near Ronda de Dalt in Horta district. The simple and functional three-storey building, shaped like a storage container, houses one of the world's largest libraries on the Second Republic, the Civil War, exile, Francoism and the transition to democracy. In the open space of the central courtyard is a reproduction of *Guernica* as exhibited in its original location.

NEARBY

MISTOS SCULPTURE ❷

In front of the pavilion stands an original sculpture, *Mistos*, a monumental book of matches by Claes Oldenburg and his wife Coosje van Bruggen. It was erected in 1992 as part of an ambitious municipal programme to endow the entire city, even the suburbs, with sculptures by well-known artists. *Mistos* is eye-catching because of its height (21 metres), but especially because it is an immediately recognizable everyday object. So it often eclipses *Guernica*, the real jewel of Vidal i Barraquer avenue.

HORTA VELLA FARM ❸

Avinguda del Cardenal Vidal i Barraquer, 15
• www.marti-codolar.net
• Open daily, 8am-10pm
• Metro: Montbau

A hidden garden

In the mid-19th century, wealthy businessman Lluís Martí i Codolar (1843–1915) bought a large property in Horta Vella la Granja as his leisure park. He soon had part of the land laid out as gardens and cultivated the rest so successfully that he was awarded the Grand Cross of the Order of Merit for Agriculture. He was also passionately keen on building up an exotic animal collection, for which he acquired various species: ostriches, flamingos, pelicans, swans, kangaroos, llamas, camels and even an Indian elephant.

In 1891, in deep financial trouble, Martí was forced to sell his collection of animals to the local authorities, thus founding Barcelona Zoo which opened on the annual festival of Our Lady of Mercy (La Mercè) in 1892. In 1946, his heirs sold the property to the religious order the Salesians of Don Bosco.

The 19th-century mansion is now a Salesian seminary, but you can ask to visit the gardens. A short walk in such a beautiful place soon reveals the reason for its success. In the past it attracted such illustrious visitors as Ferdinand VII, Alfonso XIII and Don Bosco, founder of the Salesian Order, while poets and painters, including Eduardo Marquina and Santiago Rusiñol, found inspiration for some of their work there.

The gardens are filled with a variety of plants, ancient trees, jets and fountains whose lapping water is an invitation to relax. Beautiful sculptures, such as those representing the different ages of man or the labours of Hercules, the mythical founder of Barcelona, are dotted here and there. Cigarral de la Santa, a peaceful area created in the early 20th century in honour of Saint Teresa, deserves special mention.

NEARBY

A VISUAL POEM ❹

Near Horta Velodrome, before you reach the Parc del Laberint (Labyrinth Park), there is a visual poem in three phases by the great Barcelona poet Joan Brossa (1919–98). It represents the stages of human life: birth (capital A), the vicissitudes of existence (with its points, parentheses and question marks) and death (broken A).

THE GENERAL'S WATCHTOWER

⑤

Junction of Carrer de Crehuet and Carrer de Porto
• Metro: Horta

*General
on guard*

The Horta-Guinardó district of Barcelona is perhaps the least frequented by tourists and the travelling public, yet it has many places associated with interesting anecdotes about the lives of 19th-century locals, such as General Crehuet, an old soldier who lived for many years in a manor house on Carrer de Porto.

Within the grounds was a little watchtower fitted with openings through which the general surveyed and guarded the surrounding fields. The tower, at the corner of the narrowest street in Barcelona, is still standing.

A FEW RECORDS

The narrowest street

At the junction of Carrer de Crehuet and Carrer de Porto. The street is 200 metres long, but at its narrowest point, less than 3 metres wide.

The smallest door

No. 10 Carrer del Comerç (La Ribera). Nearby, the rather romantic name of Carrer dels Petons (kisses) originates from the Middle Ages, when condemned men were allowed to say goodbye to their loved ones and receive their final embrace there.

The oldest house

No. 6 Carrer de San Doménech del Call (Barrio Gótico) was first inhabited in the 12th century. The walls have been leaning since the 1428 earthquake.

WHERE DO *ELS QUINZE* COME FROM?

In the Horta neighbourhood many premises, from the poultry merchant to the supermarket, not to mention the lottery booth, are named *Els Quinze* (The Fifteen).

This is also how people refer to part of the Guinardó district, particularly between the junction of Passeig de Maragall and Avinguda de Borbón.

The name refers to the 15 centime fare for the journey between Plaça Urquinaona and Plaça d'Ibiza. In the early 20th century, the tramways had different fares for the various routes. No. 46 cost 15 or 25 centimes, depending on the distance travelled. The conductors rang a bell and announced: *Els quinze*, so warning any passengers who might be tempted to plead ignorance and travel on free to the end of the line.

Tramway No. 46 was inaugurated in 1901 and the route closed on 20 December 1965, at which point a bar owner on Avinguda Mare de Déu de Montserrat named his premises Els Quinze.

THE HORTA WASHERWOMEN   **6**

Carrer d'Aiguafreda, 10 to 30
• Metro: Horta

*Old-style
laundry*

Strolling around Aiguafreda, one of the most typical streets in Horta-Guinardó, it is difficult to imagine that, 100 years ago, the little gardens here formed part of the biggest laundry in Barcelona.

Several metres beneath the streets of Horta-Guinardó, water ran directly from mountain streams. It was so clear and clean that it could be drunk straight from the wells that were part of each Aiguafreda house.

Over three centuries, until the Civil War, the washerwomen did their laundry first with very cold water then with hot water.

The difference in temperature, together with the purity of the water and the women's efficiency, gave the clothes an unequalled freshness and cleanliness when they were sent back to Barcelona.

One of the paradoxes of the city between the 16th and 19th centuries was that the supply of water bore little relation to citizens' needs. Wealthy people often had no water for laundry purposes, nor did they have enough space to

lay their washing out to dry.

The water also used to contain a high level of chalk, damaging the smart clothing made by famous designers of the times, much of it imported from Paris. All this contributed to the development of the Horta laundry service, which employed a great many people.

Every Monday, errand boys were responsible for collecting sacks of washing, piled up at a point between Vía Laeitana and Carrer del Consell de Cent, returning them on Fridays so that the bourgeoisie could dress up in all their finery during the weekend.

NEARBY

BARCELONA'S ONLY PARISH CEMETERY   **7**

Carrer de Saldes, 3

The small cemetery beside the church in Carrer de Nazareth is the only one under non-municipal management in Barcelona. With 1,000 plots, it still looks like a village burial ground. The tombs are those of local people, such as Manuel Carrasco y Formiguera, one of the leaders of the Catalan Nationalist party, Unió Democràtica de Catalunya, who was shot during the Civil War.

PLAQUE COMMEMORATING THE GUERRILLA ⑧ FACERÍAS

Plaça de las Madres de Plaza de Mayo
• Metro: Llucmajor

**" Anarchist
and gentleman**

At the end of the Spanish Civil War, a few thousand former Republican fighters vowed to go underground and continue the fight against Franco. Hardened anarchists and communists were trained as commandos and used to sabotage factories, railways and power grids, to raid banks and jewellers, and to carry out assassination attempts on prominent members of the regime. The frequent arrests of activists led to many imprisonments as well as death sentences from the late 1940s onwards. This weakened the movement and it was dissolved in the late 1960s. In Catalonia, the most notorious guerrillas were Wenceslao Jiménez, Marcelino Massana, Quico Sabaté, Ramon Vila Capdevila (*Caracremada* or "Burnt Face") and Josep Lluís i Facerías (alias *el Face*).

El Face (1920–57), also known as *Petronio* as well as *el Señorito,* "the Young Gentleman", because of his elegant style, campaigned from the age of 16 with the anarchist union, the National Confederation of Labour (CNT). During the war, he volunteered to fight for the militia in Aragon. He was captured in 1939 and spent several years in prison. Once released, he threw himself back into the armed struggle and pulled off coups of rare audacity, such as the attack on the Pedralbes building (21 October 1951), a brothel on the road to Esplugues used by philandering members of high society. During this incident a well-known Barcelona businessman and Franco supporter, Antonio Massana Sanjuán, was killed in bed with his underage mistress (his niece, according to popular gossip).

On 30 August 1957, *el Face* went to a rendezvous with a gang member in the Sant Andreu district, not suspecting that the police were in the know and had laid an ambush for him. He was shot by gunmen hidden in the

neighbouring buildings, with no chance of defending himself.

At the corner of Carrer del Doctor Pi i Molist in Plaça de las Madres de la Plaza de Mayo, a circular plaque next to the fountain marks the site where Facerías was shot, on 30 August 1957 at 10.45. An inscription alongside commemorates the victims of another military dictatorship, that of Argentina.

UNUSUAL GRAVES
IN SANT ANDREU CEMETERY

9

Carrer del Garrofers, 35–47
• www.cbsa.es
• Open daily, 8am-6pm
• Metro: Llucmajor or Fabra i Puig

> *Saint Andrew has his little saint too*

The entrance to the old cemetery of Saint Andrew is in Carrer del Garrofers above the Meridiana and Heron City shopping centre. Opened in 1839 in a rural setting, it is now hemmed in by buildings and avenues. Although less well known than Montjuïc or Poblenou cemeteries, Saint Andrew's features wonderful sculptures and imposing mausoleums. In Section I alone you can see the most beautiful tombs belonging to wealthy families who chose for their eternal resting place an obligatory rite of passage: just as in life, they built their homes in the busiest streets. This is notable in the Martí family tomb (1895) with its carved sarcophagus covered with roses, and the pantheon of the Benguerel family (1911), a treasure trove of Modernist architecture.

In Section III, note especially the pantheon of the Soldier (1940), where the remains of many Francoist combatants from the Civil War lie, watched over by the statue of a helmeted soldier bearing a rifle and cartridges. Before the 2010 legislation on historical memory made it obligatory to erase symbols predating the Constitution, the soldier was vandalized: his head was knocked to the ground twice and he lost his nose. Now restored and under the protection of the Constitutional insignia, he can expect to be left in peace.

The tomb of a local resident is also in this section: Ignasi Iglésias, renowned playwright of the early 20th century. Not far away, a huge bell tower of reinforced concrete shaped like a rocket is unmissable.

In a niche at the foot of the chapel that rises over Section II lies the most famous body in the cemetery: the boy *santet* of Saint Andrew, who rivals the *santet* of Poblenou in popularity (see p. 229). His name was Francesc Pla Saña and he died aged 25, in 1918. When he was a seminarian, the bishop refused to ordain him because he was the son of a spiritualist. As he was so good and helpful to everyone during his lifetime, he is still asked for favours and his statue is always covered in flowers.

KAGYU SAMYE DZONG

10

Rambla de la Montana, 97
• Tel: 93 436 2626 (10.00–13.00)
• www.samye.es
• Open Tuesday, Wednesday and Thursday, 6.30pm-8pm
• Metro: Guinardó

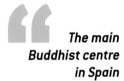

*The main
Buddhist centre
in Spain*

The main Buddhist centre in Spain was founded in 1977 by his Holiness the 16th Karmapa. It preserves and spreads the teachings of Buddha and is dedicated to the promotion of the physical, mental, and spiritual well-being of its adherents.

The centre belongs to the Tibetan order of Buddhism, Karma Kagyu, and its official name is Karma Lodrö Gyamtso Ling, which means "place of illuminated activity where an ocean of intelligence exists."

The spacious sanctuary has a little shop selling books, incense, figurines, clothes, and various objects associated with meditation and Buddhism.

From time to time, the centre is visited by Tibetan lamas who come to lead seminars on philosophy and Buddhist meditation.

In addition, they offer a variety of courses; for example, on the history of Buddhism in India, or reflections on the seven points of mental stimulation.

Other activities include film shows, yoga classes, courses on different therapies, and the organization of spiritual retreats in the mountains around Barcelona.

In farms far from the city, various types of retreats take place, intended for beginners as well as long-term practitioners. Those aspiring to become lamas undertake retreats lasting at least three years.

There are also weekend retreats, such as that at Ñung-Ne, which develop compassion, one of the five elements by which pupils learn to recognize the play of energy in body and mind; or the meditational retreat, Shiné, which cultivates internal calm.

KARMA KAGYU

The Kagyu lineage is one of the four principal schools of Tibetan Buddhism, the three others being Nyingma, Sakya, and Gelug. The origins of the Kagyu school go back to the teachings of the Indian mystics Tilopa and Naropa, introduced to Tibet by the translator Marpa. Other grand masters of meditation, such as Milarepa, Gampopa, and Rechungpa, are also associated with this lineage.

The Kagyu method is based on the doctrine of Mahamudra (Great Seal) and on meditation. Currently the school has hundreds of centres around the world.

TURÓ DE LA ROVIRA

⓫

Parc dels Tres Turons
• Bus : 24, 28, 86, 119

> *Remains of the Horta anti-aircraft battery*

Offering a superb 360° panorama, Horta's anti-aircraft battery is the best viewpoint in Barcelona. Paradoxically, it was in this marvellous setting that one of the worst episodes of the Civil War took place, the Republican troops having fought to the death here against their Nationalist foes.

Their heroic resistance was even cited as an example by Winston Churchill in 1940, just before the Blitz: "I do not at all underrate the severity of the ordeal which lies before us; but I believe our countrymen will show themselves capable of standing up to it, like the brave men of Barcelona."

The air raids by Italian and German forces, supporting Franco's army by systematically bombing the civilian population, destroyed the city. In all, there were 385 raids that dropped 1,500 tons of bombs, resulting in 1,903 conflagrations that killed over 2,700 people.

In addition to Turó de la Rovira, the town has defences against air raids at Turó del Carmel, Sant Pere Mártir, Tibidabo, Montjuïc, Barceloneta, and Poblenou.

The weaponry consisted of a few anti-aircraft guns and a small fleet of planes, not enough to halt the great offensive. The guns used were mostly of English origin, Vickers 105s built in 1923.

The two types of fighter plane that were most successful in discouraging enemy attacks were the Polikarpov I-15 (nicknamed "the seagull") and I-16 ("the fly"). Both of these Soviet aircraft were acrobatic and versatile, but their guns were not very powerful.

Today, the vestiges of the anti-aircraft battery at Turó de la Rovira and the air-raid shelter have deteriorated because of lack of maintenance and the fact that, until the early 21st century, the surrounding neighbourhood was a shanty town. The authorities have launched a project to safeguard this site of great historical interest, however.

THE CARRER DE SÒCRATES BOMB ⑫

• Metro: Sant Andreu

Souvenir of a bombardment

In the working-class district of Sant Andreu, which was a village on the outskirts of Barcelona until 1897, a bomb can be seen embedded in the façade of a Modernist building at the junction of Carrer Gran de Sant Andreu and Carrer de Sòcrates.

This missile dates from September 1843, when troops under the command of Colonel Joan Prim suppressed a popular insurrection against the conservative government in Madrid, known as the "Jamància" because many of the volunteers enlisted only for the food (*jamar* is the Romany word for "eat"). As a reward for his courage, Prim was promoted to general and later became president of the Spanish government (1869–1870).

Prim's artillery bombardment of Sant Andreu inflicted a great deal of damage, but not all of the missiles exploded. The owner of the building on this street corner has kept one of them as a trophy. During a restoration project in the early 20th century, the bomb was set into the wall to commemorate these events.

NEARBY

GARDENS IN CARRER DE GRAU ⑬

Between Carrer d'Agustí i Milá and Carrer Gran de Sant Andreu is a street that harks back to an earlier age with its low houses and gardens. At No. 41 you can see a curious collection of multicoloured ceramics, representing some of the sites in the neighbourhood and around Barcelona in a naive style.

LA PRIMITIVA, BAR & ORNITHOLOGICAL SOCIETY

⑭

Avinguda Meridiana, 157
• Tel: 93 347 5520
• Open Tuesday to Sunday, 9.30am-11.30pm
• Metro: Clot

*Beer
among
the birds*

La Primitiva bar and ornithological society opened its doors over 100 years ago and little has changed since. You only have to glance at the shabby walls, the calendars several decades out of date, and the rickety furniture to appreciate the dilapidated state of the place.

Don Antonio, a canary and finch enthusiast, decided to found an ornithological society that welcomed both birds and their owners to either chat or sing.

Over the years, La Primitiva has become a meeting place for the members of this exclusive club of bird fanciers, who come to the bar for an aperitif, a coffee, or a beer, and to play dominoes or cards. Their average age is 60, but this does not detract from the lively atmosphere that promises an original way of passing time.

Every Saturday, birdsong contests are organized on the patio behind the premises. To take part, you only need to pay €12 a year and to keep a canary.

One of the great benefits of belonging to the society is that members' birds can sleep in the bar, so the little creatures are less lonely and will learn to sing along with their friends ...

Even though the bar may seem to be exclusively for men, it is open to everyone.

UNIÓN DE CANARICULTORES DE BARCELONA ⑮

Avigunda Meridiana, 91
• Tel: 93 232 4204
• www.canariosbarcelona.org
• Open Monday, Wednesday, Friday and Saturday, 6pm-9pm
• Metro: Clot

*Karaoke
for canaries*

The Barcelona canary-fanciers' union, set up seventy-five years ago, organizes an annual song competition for 1,200 canaries.

On the day of the contest, as the birds are more at ease singing in the dark, they are separated and their cages covered with a black cloth. This club of canary fanciers is also the ideal place to find advice on how to improve their song.

A canary imitates other sounds, so if it hears a CD playing first-class songs, its own performance will probably improve. Similarly, if a poor performer is placed next to a good one, the learner will soon make progress.

The annual competition has three classes: song, colour, and carriage. There are three different styles of birdsong to be judged: timbrado espagnol, roller, and malinois.

As for the colour and carriage contests, the most impressive thing about the show is that you can see for yourself the endless genetic variations between birds.

Some canaries have extravagant feathering and crests, while those entered in the colour class flaunt all the colours of the rainbow.

MONUMENT TO THE METRE

16

Meridian Arc
Plaça de les Glòries Catalanes
• Metro: Glòries or Monumental

The role of Barcelona in the definition of the metre, in 1792

Plaça de les Glòries Catalanes was chosen as the site of a monument commemorating the 200th anniversary of the measurement of the terrestrial meridian, which was used to determine the length of the metre. The inauguration ceremony took place before work on the surrounding site was completed, because time was running out for the launch of the 1992 Olympic Games in Barcelona. The 40-metre steel monument, the work of François Scali and Alain Domingo and known as the Meridian Arc, represents the orographic profile (i.e. showing the terrain's relief), to scale, of the distance between Dunkirk and Barcelona. There is a reason for the length of 40 metres: under the new system, the Earth's total circumference as measured along the terrestrial meridians (or lines of longitude) running from North Pole to South Pole was defined as 40 million metres (or 40,000 kilometres). Beyond being a tribute to the metre as a system of measurement, the arc is dedicated to all the scientists involved in the definition of the metre using primitive instruments, in particular Jean-Baptiste Delambre and Pierre-François Méchain. On one side of the monument is an inscription describing their work.

THE DEFINITION OF THE METRE SINCE 1791

Surprisingly enough, the word "metre" has only been in existence for a little over two centuries. Before it came into being, there was no standard measurement for calculating distances: hands, feet, or other local units were used. In 1790, the French National Assembly proposed a universal measurement standard, based on natural phenomena and therefore acceptable to all nations. The chosen measurement was 1/10,000,000 of the quadrant of the Earth's circumference (from the North Pole through Paris to the Equator), to be known as the metre (from the Greek word metron, meaning "measure"). Because it was impossible to measure the entire quarter of the meridian, the solution adopted was to measure part of it and calculate the total. The meridian arc chosen was that between Dunkirk and Barcelona. After several years of work, a platinum bar was made in 1799. This standard metre, today symbolic (although no longer accurate), is preserved at the Bureau International des Poids et Mesures (International Bureau of Weights and Measures) in Sèvres (France). In 1875, seventeen countries signed the Metre Convention. In 1889, the Conférence Générale des Poids et Mesures sanctioned a platinum/iridium alloy prototype of the metre that would not be subject to any variations in length. Since the 20th century, technology has allowed the metre to be defined with extreme precision but has also made it very difficult for the general public to understand.

For more information on the origin of the metre, the methods used to calculate it and the role of Barcelona in this scientifc adventure, see p. 156.

MUSEU DE CORROSSES FÚNEBRES

Carrer de Sancho de Ávila, 2
- Tel: 902 076 902
- Open Monday to Friday, 10am-1pm and 4pm-6pm, Saturday, 10am-1pm
- Metro: Marina

Transport to the afterlife

The Hearse Museum is not recommended for sensitive souls. Located in the basement of a branch of the municipal funerary services, it has a collection of various types of carriage and funeral cars from the 19th and 20th centuries.

This is a strange, damp, and rather improbable place. It displays all kinds of conveyances for the deceased, from those decked out in white for children and adolescents to Gothic carriages in the so-called "French" style. Most come complete with mannequins elegantly dressed for the occasion, some in white and others in black. The same applies to the horses, featuring an array of funerary ornaments typical of their day.

Although the set pieces are very well done, it is a pity that the space is so restricted. Nevertheless, there are about twenty vehicles, some drawn by model horses, and showcases displaying the outfits of employees and horses in funerary procession.

This lugubrious, even melodramatic, atmosphere is heightened by the presence of an immense carriage entirely lined in black cloth. This was intended for widows who could afford to pay for lavish funerals, which were mainly reserved for officials or wealthy people, the rare exceptions being burials during Holy Week or at Christmas.

Other striking vehicles include a Studebaker and a 1976 Buick, both of which suggest a less formal style of funeral.

A close look at the exhibits also reveals many symbols linked to death, both in the hearses and on the employees' uniforms. For example, the Greek letters alpha and omega, which symbolize the beginning and the end. Also note the figure of an owl, a symbol of solitude, silence, and death, or that of Athena, the Greek goddess of wisdom, whom we are supposed to meet in the next world.

If you want to know more about the death industry, Barcelona's funerary services also run a coffin factory, which you can visit by special arrangement, although it is not normally open to the public.

DIPÒSIT DE LES AIGÜES ⑱

Pompeu Fabra University
Carrer de Ramón Trías Fargas, 39
• Tel: 93 542 1709
• Open Monday to Friday, 8am-1pm, Saturday, 8am-2pm
• Metro: Ciutadella Vila Olímpica

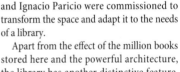

One of the best-kept architectural secrets in Barcelona

The Dipòsit de les Aigües (Water Deposit) is one of the best-kept architectural secrets of the city. The building, inspired by the Mirabilis Roman baths, was constructed in 1880 by the architect Josep Fontserè. It was designed as a reservoir for water, hence the vaulted ceilings and brick walls resting on forty-eight pillars.

But over the years it has been used as a retirement home, a fire service warehouse, a film studio, an improvized hospital during the war, and finally, a university library.

In the 1970s, Pompeu Fabra University bought the building, thinking that it was an ideal opportunity to expand its facilities. Architects Lluís Clotet and Ignacio Paricio were commissioned to transform the space and adapt it to the needs of a library.

Apart from the effect of the million books stored here and the powerful architecture, the library has another distinctive feature. Silence is of course the norm, but if you listen carefully, the roaring of lions and tigers can be heard through the huge windows. This is no illusion, the library is next door to Barcelona Zoo.

NEARBY

TÀPIES' CONTEMPLATION ROOM

In Pompeu Fabra University, a few metres from the library, is a very strange "contemplation room." In this lay chapel, there are no saints or gods to be worshipped, but simply two canvases: Díptic de la campana and Serp i plat, both works by Antoni Tàpies.

This room, designed by the Catalan sculptor and painter, contains some twenty chairs fixed to the wall.

The original idea was to create a space where visitors could come to terms with themselves, call upon a personal deity, or just admire two brilliant works by Tàpies in absolute silence. If you would like to visit this meditative space, just ask permission at reception.

POBLENOU CEMETERY

20

Carrer de Carmen Amaya
- Tel: 93 225 1661
- Open daily, 9am-6pm
- Metro: Poblenou
- *The Kiss of Death*: division 3
- *El Santet*: division 1, inner plot 4

Kiss of death

*T*he Kiss of Death is one of the strangest tombs in the Poblenou cemetery. In this masterpiece by J. Barba, a winged death's head is simply kissing the forehead of the deceased. The marble sculpture is a tribute to a dead son. In 1991, it was one of the works most commented on in a Berlin exhibition on the theme of eroticism (!).

El Santet is another strange tomb, with an improvised altar carrying the most surrealist offerings to be seen in the cemetery, such as coffee caramels, cigarettes, and throat pastilles.

Francesc Canals Ambrós (Barcelona, 1879–899), known as "El Santet," was killed in an accident just before his twentieth birthday. Shortly afterwards, the rumour arose that El Santet granted people's prayers. From then on, the number of believers grew and grew, and his tomb is now always covered in flowers and other offerings.

Behind the walls of the Poblenou cemetery, over 5 metres high, lies a good part of the history of 19th-century Barcelona. The "old cemetery," as the locals call it, is embedded in a traditional neighbourhood that is beginning to give way to modern buildings. It lies almost opposite one of the beaches most popular with young people, Mar Bella.

The cemetery was opened in 1775 in an attempt to solve public sanitation problems. Although now within the urban area, it was originally some distance from the city, outside the walls.

The old cemetery brings together various architectural and aesthetic styles arranged in almost chronological order, and provides a wonderful opportunity to gain some understanding of the personalities and events of another age.

NEARBY

"LITTLE FRANCE"

21

This small and friendly neighbourhood, home to the Palo Alto Foundation, is known as Little France (França Xica), because over 150 years ago, a large number of French employees of a major steelworks settled here. Many of the buildings from that time, however, have been pulled down for housing development projects, although a few streets of rather dilapidated charm remain, such as Carrers de Pellaires and de Ferrers.

THE WATER TOWER SUICIDE

Plaça de Ramón Calsina
• Metro: Selva de Mar

*Not fit
for use ...*

Designed in 1882 by the architect Pere Falqués, this historic monument has a macabre story associated with it. One detail was overlooked in the construction of the tower, intended to supply drinking water – the proximity of the sea allowed salt water to infiltrate ...

The project was a failure and the devastated investor who had backed it threw himself from the top of the tower.

The system never worked properly and so has remained a monument to human error, inspiring the artists Josep María Subirachs and Ramón Calsina, after whom the square is named.

This tower is important, however, as a tribute to the industrialization of Catalonia and the efforts expended by the workers of the time.

It also forms part of a project to recover the symbols of industrialization. Over the years, it has become a landmark for the local residents, a playground for the children, and a silent witness to the urban transformation that has taken place, with ever more new buildings under construction.

OTHER RESERVOIRS THAT HAVE SURVIVED THE RAVAGES OF TIME ...

Water towers are used to store water from underground springs or brought in by pipes.

Their height facilitates distribution of the water, sometimes using a pump and sometimes by force of gravity alone. A great many of these towers, most of which date from the early 20th century, have been preserved as monuments to Barcelona's industrial heritage rather than serving their original function.

One of the most remarkable, and the highest (53 m), of these towers is at Tibidabo.

At No. 98 Passeig de Fabra i Puig stands a water tower built in 1910, the property of the Canyelles water company. Nearby, in the Rambla de Sant Andreu, is one of the oldest towers (1853).

Carrer de Peris i Mancheta is home to a water tower built by Josep Oriol (see p. 139), which supplied a journalists' cooperative on Carrer de Roger de Llúria.

NEARBY

PALO ALTO FOUNDATION
Carrer dels Pellaires, 30
• Metro: Selva de Mar

This unusual space, an industrial complex dating from 1875, was renovated in 1987 by Pierre Roca and now houses a foundation dedicated to creative design. The original aim was to avoid destroying the former factories and convert them into spacious, well-lit studios where various artists could work. One of the tenants is the designer Javier Mariscal, whose drawings have appeared on the cover of magazines such as the *New Yorker* and *EPS*. The Mariscal studio employs a team of over forty designers. The Palo Alto Foundation has also served as the setting for the film *El Embrujo de Shanghai* (The Shanghai Spell), directed by Fernando Trueba and starring Ariadna Gil.

THE STONE THAT MARKS AN ANCIENT BOUNDARY
Parque Carlos I

A symbolic stone in the Carlos I park, between Carrer de Marina and Carrer del Doctor Trueta, is in fact one of the boundary stones that used to mark the limits of the municipalities of Sant Martí and Barcelona. The inscription "B i SM" engraved on the stone recalls its original function.

The former village of Sant Martí de Provençals was annexed by Barcelona in 1897.

Vast factories installed themselves in the district, earning it the nickname "Catalonian Manchester."

ALTERNATIVE CONTEMPORARY ART
Hangar
Passatge del Marqués de Santa Isabel, 40
• Tel: 93 308 4041
• Open Monday to Friday, 9am-2pm
• Metro: Poblenou

The Hangar design centre is located at Can Ricart, an industrial site conceived in the mid-19th century by the architect Josep Oriol y Bernardet. Of the former factory, only a few abandoned buildings remain. Some 250 metres from the entrance, in one of the vast units scattered throughout this phantom space, Hangar set up shop ten years ago and has already survived a fire and several eviction threats. The centre keeps going thanks to the support of the artists' collective, which hopes by this type of venture to prevent property speculation. In fact, after a long fight to establish its rights, it now enjoys the recognition and support of the local authorities.

A visit to Hangar will let you see the latest trends in Barcelona's arts scene and the works of invited artists from all round the world.

SOCIEDAD COLOMBÓFILA DE BARCELONA ㉖

Passeig del Taulat, 7
• Tel: 93 266 0210
• Metro: Poblenou
Federación Catalana de Colombicultura
Córsega, 681, entresol 3°
• Metro: Diagonal
• Tel: 93 436 2203

*The world
of pigeons*

For over eighty years, the Barcelona pigeon-fanciers club and federation have been breeding pigeons.

The society, with its homing pigeons, and the federation, with its racing birds, are almost exclusively for men. They organize outdoor activities and meetings that revolve around the world of pigeons. Racing pigeons are by definition aggressive birds: nervous, resilient, and tireless. They are also courtship experts.

Homing pigeons, on the other hand, have very different traits. They are more docile, friendly, and always return to their lofts.

They also have a more athletic body shape. Their breeding and training is very different from that of racing pigeons as they develop an instinct for orientation rather than speed.

The skills of the two types of bird are tested in spring and summer.

HOMING PIGEONS

Whether released at distances of 500 m or 100 km, and in certain cases, even over 1,000 km, the homing pigeon has the fantastic ability to always find its way back home. Although the reason for this exceptional skill is still unknown, some people attribute the pigeons' gift to the presence of tiny crystals in the brain. This trait was detected a long time ago, notably by Julius Caesar who used homing pigeons in his invasion of Gaul to send messages back to Rome and inform his followers of the campaign's progress.

On the other hand, make no mistake: there is no such thing as the pigeon you sometimes see in films, which is released to take a message somewhere and then returns. The pigeon is only (so to speak) capable of journeying homewards. This is why, in order to send a message to several different places, pigeons raised at each destination have to be taken out. To carry several successive messages to the same place, the requisite number of pigeons would be needed ... There's nothing at all miraculous about this, and moving pigeons from one loft to another will make it difficult to pick up your messages ...

ALPHABETICAL INDEX

ALPHABETICAL INDEX